BARBARA SYKES'
TRAINING
Border Collies

BARBARA SYKES'
TRAINING
Border Collies

BARBARA SYKES

THE CROWOOD PRESS

First published in 2014 by
The Crowood Press Ltd
Ramsbury, Marlborough
Wiltshire SN8 2HR

www.crowood.com

This impression 2017

British Library Cataloguing-in-Publication Data
A catalogue record for this book is available from the British Library.

ISBN 978 1 84797 889 9

Dedication
To all the Border Collies in my life from childhood to present day who have taught me so much about patience, understanding and the value of friendship. From being my confidantes as a child, to being there for my children as they grew up and always being by my side through the dark times, I thank each and every one of you for the precious times we have shared.

Acknowledgements
I would like to thank Ian and Lucy for their expertise in taking photographs that can tell a story, Gemma and Ben for their help and patience, and special thanks to Diane Jones for all her help and support.

Photographs supplied by Ian Hughes, Lucy Pearson and the author.

Typeset by Jean Cussons Typesetting, Diss, Norfolk

Printed and bound in Malaysia by Times Offset (M) Sdn Bhd

CONTENTS

INTRODUCTION

At the end of Chapter 1 is a dedication to the Border Collie as a breed, and when I started to write this Introduction I couldn't stop thinking about some of the words it contains: honesty, integrity, loyalty, friend and partner – words that really do sum up an exceptional and very special breed of dog. So special, in fact, that I believe it is important to understand as much as possible about their history and about the ancestors of today's Border Collies, which is why I refer to their working instincts and to the shepherds who first gave us this amazing breed. There is a notion that a dog from working lines will not make a good companion but a collie bred from compatible working breed lines is a true Border Collie and will have the temperament, intelligence and loyalty to be a perfect companion, a working dog, or both, as long as he is understood. This book is about training by understanding the instincts, the different characteristics of the variations in the breed and communication. Once you can understand what your dog is thinking, and why he is thinking it, training him will become much easier. But he needs to be able to understand you, and repeated commands or words he doesn't recognize will confuse him, whereas a carefully thought-out movement of your body will explain to him in a few short seconds what wasted minutes of misunderstood words can fail to do.

Throughout the book I use the term 'guardian', as the word 'owner' does not sit well with me; we don't own our children, we parent them, and no matter how much money may be exchanged for our dogs, we parent and protect them rather than own them. Border Collies need a leader

---

A NOTE ON 'TLC' – THINKING LIKE CANINES

TLC – Thinking Like Canines – is a home-grown ideology based on years of living with Border Collies and studying their interactions with each other and with people, and honed by allowing them to teach me how to have a better understanding not only of them as a breed but of every other breed of dog I encounter. Rather than having a pre-set idea of how a dog should be trained, and what he should or should not do, the concept of asking the dog what he would like and how he would like to be trained, and of seeing the world through his eyes instead of purely through our own, takes us on an amazing journey to discover not only *what* dogs are thinking but *why*.

Training is not about demanding, or even requesting; it's about co-operation, and discovering how a relationship can change from man and dog to a true partnership through communication. Thinking Like Canines is about studying each dog as an individual and asking nothing from him but the four marks of respect that he learns from his mother and which he easily recognizes and understands. Dogs by nature are givers, not takers, and TLC is about us learning to converse with and understand them, rather than expecting them to do everything our way. When you study your dog closely, watch his body language, know what he is going to do before he does it, can feel his every emotion and can sit with him quietly, allowing him to simply be himself, you have a true partnership – a bond that enables you to converse without words but by simply thinking like a canine.

and, whether the term used is pack leader or parent, if not provided a collie will feel lost and unprotected. Pack leaders are not dominant, they do not revel in submission and they do not harm or bully their subordinates; a true leader is a parent with responsibilities, who guides, protects and nurtures – if they don't, they become bullies. No dog should ever be submissive but nor should he become dominant; each dog is different, and has distinctive characteristics, and to get a happy, balanced collie the training and communication needs to be equally well balanced.

I am often asked whether it is easier to train male or female Border Collies, but it's not about gender – it's about the dog's nature. By taking a journey back in time in the first two chapters to meet his ancestors, you will have fun working out the character of your own Collie before you start training him. (The word 'He' is used throughout the book as a generic term, as another of my foibles is not to call a dog 'it' unless in a sentence giving general information.)

This book is written purely and simply for the understanding and basic training of Border Collies, to help you to have a well-mannered dog you can be proud to call your best friend.

BORDER COLLIE FACTS AND TIPS

Facts
- Chasing is not a Border Collie instinct but if they are encouraged to do so, rather than discouraged, it will develop into a bad habit
- Border Collies do not round up children thinking they are sheep; they are interacting and playing as they would with each other
- Border Collies do not need hours of exercise; they need a sensible amount of exercise, a calming diet and company
- Border Collies are not naturally hyperactive but excessive ball-throwing or repetitive games that over-excite them can lead to hyperactivity
- Border Collies are very stoic but they are also very sensitive and anything that causes them stress can affect them for a long time

- Border Collies respond to communication and company, which they can never get enough of, and they love the challenge of a game that makes them think, but over-stimulation of mind and body can lead to behavioural problems, particularly if the dog is then left to try to wind down on his own
- Border Collies are amazing companions and they don't need to be 'doing things' all the time
- Border Collies are the masters of downtime and can switch from active to resting very quickly but if they are kept active all the time they will forget how to relax.

Tips
- Playing games with a ball that include working out a problem, such as hide and seek or waiting before retrieving, will exercise the mind as well as the body and discourage chasing
- Teaching a child to play gentle interactive games, and making sure that games don't develop into chasing, can change the relationship between dog and child from competition to companionship
- Walking with a Border Collie and sharing special moments is one of the best parts of exercise and keeps a dog focused, but any strenuous exercise should always finish with quality time together
- Border Collies that become hyperactive may also be on a diet that is too high in energy; reducing the energy in the food and introducing games that make him think rather get over-excited can help to calm him down
- Border Collies need to understand what is wanted of them; if you are unsure how to respond to any behavioural trait or problem, take time to think through why it happened as an incorrect response made in haste could take some time to rectify
- Border Collies love to please and rarely refuse to do something they are asked to do, so before they become stressed or over-stimulated with a game, slow things down and spend time just enjoying their company
- If you have more than one dog, try to spend

some quality time or have special moments with each of them individually; they love human companionship, and when you have them on their own, even for just a few moments, you discover little traits you don't notice when they are together

- Border Collies need time to relax and switch off, but if they are not encouraged to do this they will be in permanent overdrive. Make sure they have a place of their own that is peaceful and quiet, where they can go and rest; even young dogs need time out.

1 MEET YOUR BORDER COLLIE

Life with a Border Collie is rarely dull and is often full of surprises. One minute they are full of fun and bounding around and then, in the wink of an eye, they have engaged their working brain and become focused, almost to the point of appearing to be in a trance. However, appearances can be deceptive and even when a Border Collie appears to have 'switched off' his brain is usually ticking away, working out his next move.

Originally bred as working dogs, they were often required to diversify into different areas of the same kind of work. The working life of a sheepdog often consists of gathering sheep into the fields from the hills and then driving them back again at the end of the day. He may be called upon to shed, or separate, a small group of sheep from the main flock, or even cut out a single sheep from the flock and keep it apart until the shepherd can catch it. He needs gentleness and patience to handle ewes and lambs, and a brave heart to tackle a stubborn ram. One dog rarely excels at all areas of shepherding work, although Collies will certainly try their best, but this wonderful breed does sometimes have to admit that, as good as they are, they just can't be brilliant at everything.

So a shepherd with a variety of tasks will usually have several Collies, each one a specialist in his own field. These dogs may all appear to be the same – fun-loving, hard-working little dogs – but each one carries different traits through his genes – traits that may still be apparent in Collies that aren't working. For example, a Collie who prefers to 'fix' his gaze on something moving, rather than move with it, probably comes from a line of dogs with a strong 'eye' – a trait that can be managed once it is understood. A shepherd trying to catch a sheep will become very frustrated if the sheep moves every time he is within reach of it and his dog moves with it. In contrast, a dog with a strong 'eye' will stare at the sheep, almost hypnotizing it, thus enabling the shepherd to move in closer and catch it. But the dog that moves with the sheep also has an important role to play: a strong-eyed dog may cause distress to a ewe with lambs at foot, while a dog who is willing to move with the ewe and gentle her back into the fold becomes an important team member.

A shepherd with a small flock would have only one dog, which would soon become a jack of all trades, although probably only excelling at one. If he chose to have two dogs, he would make sure that their strongest traits were different, thus ensuring that not only was he gaining a more diverse team but he was also making it easier for each dog. A shepherd with a large flock of sheep may have several dogs, and, rather than try to force any of them into a line of work to which they were not best suited, he would observe

A Border Collie working sheep will be able to separate one sheep from the flock without becoming over-excited or losing his temper.

A strong dog with a 'good eye' can almost hypnotize a sheep with his gaze, and he must be brave enough to keep the sheep still until the shepherd can get close enough to catch it.

ing dogs, who might not have been as reliable at gathering, but could be depended upon to make sure the sheep were driven back to their upper grazing lands. The outrunning dogs might not be as strong at pushing the sheep away back up the hills, but they would support and help the dogs that were.

THE COLLIE 'EYE'

With this background knowledge of the breed we can see how they all have different attributes, each of which needs to be recognized to enable us to understand how to manage any problems that may arise during training. For example, a dog with a strong 'eye' may sit for hours just staring at a ball that isn't moving or he may fix his gaze on another dog. This can become an obsession, which in itself can create more problems, but once we understand why the dog is doing it, then it is much easier to manage by making sure each 'fixation' is curbed, first of all by removing him from the object of fascination, and then by giving him something to do that breaks his concentration. A dog with less 'eye' will soon become tired of something that doesn't move and will either try to make it move, or will move on to something more interesting. This isn't a new or unusual trait for a Border Collie and a shepherd with just one dog would manage it at

them, noting which trait each dog favoured. They would all be trained to work separately, but as part of a team each one would have a specific role. They would all be sent to gather the flock from the hills but the best outrunning dogs would be the ones he relied upon to make sure all the sheep were gathered in. However, when it came to 'driving' them back up the hill, he would rely more on the strength of his driv-

A dog driving sheep away from the shepherd will work lower to the ground than a dog 'holding' a sheep with his gaze, his strength being in his powerful movement and self-confidence.

the start of the training process. He needs a dog with a strong eye, but too much eye can cause problems when working with a flock of sheep, so he would encourage the young dog to keep moving with the sheep rather than using his favoured trait. The most important aspect for any shepherd training his dogs is to make sure they are balanced. Several dogs can balance each other when working, but a single dog must have all his traits brought into balance so he learns to pay less attention to his favoured trait, and more to the less favoured ones.

The last thing a shepherd needs is for any of his dogs to 'worry' or try to kill his sheep. His dogs need to be brave but able to exercise control, and they must stay calm no matter how stressful the situation. A sheepdog that becomes frustrated or over-excited loses focus and concentration, and in so doing not only makes the job more difficult but can make mistakes that might cost the shepherd some sheep – or even his job.

We are now beginning to get a picture of how diverse the breed can be. The Border Collie is an intelligent dog who will work quite happily on his own but is an equally capable team player, balancing his strongest trait with those he is working with. However, whether working alone or as part of a team, a Border Collie still needs a mentor. Without someone he trusts and feels safe with, who gives him boundaries

to learn from, he will be forced to make his own decisions. Border Collies can be obsessive when they find something they enjoy doing, and they will happily work all day and every day – which provides a shepherd with a very willing workforce but can cause problems in a pet home. A Collie who learns to chase a ball before he learns how to control his enthusiasm can become ball-obsessed. A Collie who learns how to invent his own game with a ball, before running to retrieve one, will be less obsessive, and will be able to amuse himself without getting over-excited.

DECISION-MAKERS

Max was sent to bring home a small group of ewes and lambs that had strayed from the main flock. One very stubborn mum refused to return, stamping her feet at him each time he tried to move her and her lamb. Max left her, gathered together the more manageable strays and returned them to the main flock. Max's shepherd didn't berate him for failing to bring them all back; instead he told him he was a good lad and watched with a smile on his face as Max disappeared. Almost half an hour later Max returned with the wayward ewe and her lamb. He had gone back for her and patiently kept adjusting his distance behind her, allowing her freedom to move but only in the direction he wanted her to go. Max worked out what he needed to do, made a decision, and his shepherd trusted him implicitly. This was a combination of good breeding, good training and complete trust in one another.

THE DIVERSE BORDER COLLIE

Just as Border Collies are diverse in their capabilities, so they are in their appearance, and with each variation of coat colour, length and texture come different characteristics and personalities. Making the breed even more fascinating, the very set of the ears and the colour of the eyes can tell us a great deal about each individual dog.

A dog with a strong eye can become obsessive about focusing on one sheep so is encouraged to stay on the move in order to keep its working traits in balance.

The shepherd's choice for working in all weathers and ground conditions would be a short-coated collie, as the short coat sheds water and doesn't get matted with mud. These are often high-stamina collies, usually with a strong eye.

In order to understand the different types and characteristics, we need to know which field of expertise each type of collie would have specialized in, and the reason behind the breeding. A shepherd needing his dog to work all year round, in all weathers and often on muddy ground, would prefer a short-coated dog. If the dog is expected to work at a distance, and perhaps in strong winds, he would prefer a dog with pricked ears. To be able to 'hold' a sheep with his gaze until his master arrives on the scene, a dog needs to be bold and to have a good strong 'eye' – this eye may be lighter than most and often amber in colour. Over the years of breeding for specific types of work, different strains in the breed have developed. A much larger dog is required for working cattle, while small agile dogs are often better for nipping in and out of sheep-yards or running over rough ground. A very big and heavy Collie may soon tire when doing hill work but will be able to stand his ground in a yard full of sheep, whereas a lighter Collie will have little trouble running up and down steep hills. Thus it is easy to understand why a shepherd with a large flock of sheep would want more than one dog.

It wasn't just a case of ensuring he had enough dogs to work the flock, but of making sure he had all the skills in his team to meet every demand of the job. Little could our ancestral shepherds have dreamed that the dogs they were breeding all those years ago would go on to be just as diverse in our modern world. But all these different characteristics place demands on each of us as handlers, not only to recognize the different types of Collie but to understand how to manage them.

It is probably because Border Collies were originally bred to be so diverse in their line of work that they are able to adapt to the many different lifestyles they are in today, from work and sheepdog trialling to search and rescue and sniffer dogs, from the disciplines such as agility and obedience to the wonderful companions they have always been. The Border Collie was originally described as the shepherd's work-

---

SHEPHERD'S COMMENT: 'MY TEAM'

'If I have six different dogs, to get optimum performance I must be six different men when I am working with them. A Border Collie may not be used for working sheep but if his character and ancestral traits are recognized, it is easier to understand him.'

A Collie's idea of cooling off and getting clean at the end of a working day is a DIY bath in the horse-trough.

Then, with their wicked sense of humour, the Collie eye is used to target the nearest person to shake any excess water over!

ing companion, but we need to remember that the shepherds who gave us this breed are not the shepherds we see today. The modern shepherd has a much faster pace of life, and the use of tractors, modern sheep-handling equipment and quad bikes often means there is time left over in each working day for other jobs. In fact, few of today's shepherds are employed solely to look after sheep and the last half century has seen them becoming jacks of all trades, like the dogs they are working with. The shepherds of yesteryear would rise at dawn and, armed with sandwiches and a flask, they would start their working day with their dogs and would not return from the hills until dusk. Their dogs were not just part of their work – they were their companions, they understood each other, could almost think for each other and they were a large part of each other's lives. These men revered their dogs, breeding them for compatibility, stability and temperament; they knew which type of Collie was best suited to which kind of job, and the only time the dogs left the shepherd's feet was to work. At the end of the working day, before the shepherd saw to his own needs, his dogs were given a warm meal and settled down for the night, and on retiring they could have the freedom of the farm and the farmhouse. In some ways it sounds an almost enviable lifestyle but, like many jobs, it had its drawbacks; the winters especially would have been very hard for both men and dogs, although working in adverse conditions probably served only to strengthen their relationship.

Finding out more about the different characters within the breed is a little like a 'Who's who' of the Border Collie world. A person living with a medium-coated black and white Collie, with mid-brown coloured eyes and ears that tip over at the top, may be totally bewildered when they meet someone who has a short-coated, prick-eared, tri-coloured (black and white with brown markings), amber-eyed Collie and is at their wit's end trying to keep up with it, both mentally and physically. But even if they are both feeding their dogs the same diet, and training them in the same way, one of them will almost certainly be having problems. One dog needs to be kept very calm and is better on low-energy food. One of them will be able to display a huge amount of excitement, maybe play with a ball and then settle down for a nap, whereas the other will be excited most of the time, go into overdrive at the very thought of a ball, will chase anything it sees and struggles to be calm. But how can we tell which dog is going to be which and what makes them so different?

Prick ears and amber eyes

Border Collies are sensitive souls, and few are more so than the short-coated, prick-eared Collie with amber eyes. The amber eye can hypnotize a sheep, keeping it immobile while the shepherd moves close enough to catch it, and with this

An amber-eyed, tri-coloured, short-coated Border Collie. Typically, such dogs are usually protective of their space, don't like people staring at them, can hear sounds from a great distance and can be very sensitive.

information we can understand why an amber-eyed Collie rarely likes people he doesn't know in his space. He will often seek out someone's gaze and then fall out with them for looking back at him. People looking at him, or meeting his gaze, represents to him the challenge he issues to a sheep, so when someone moves into his space and stares at him he will feel threatened. Initially he may respond by retreating, but if this doesn't stop the unwelcome advances he will stand his ground, often issuing a growl. He is rarely timid to the point of being submissive and, if not understood, any nervous aggression that develops as a result of being made to feel vulnerable could soon become a more dominant form of aggression.

Amber eyes, which can be found in Collies of any colour and with any set of ears, must not be confused with the more yellow and much softer eye. The amber (or tiger) eye is almost transparent in appearance when compared to the yellow eye, which is much softer. Although the yellow eye is still a strong hypnotic eye with sheep, these dogs are rarely as protective of their fight or flight distance (*see* Box).

Prick-eared Collies can hear the smallest sounds from over great distances, which makes them very sensitive to, and aware of, the sounds and movements immediately around them. When working, these dogs can hear the bleat of a lost sheep when the sound is inaudible to the shepherd. Very few Border Collies have ears that flop over as their ears are vital to their ability to work at great distances from their handlers.

The short-coated Collie

The short-coated Collie with darker eyes is more inclined to retreat if feeling threatened, and can soon become very nervous to the point of being submissive. However, this dog can often bounce up to the other end of the scale if fed a diet in excess of his needs and is over-stimulated, and can become hyperactive, often behaving irrationally and seemingly tirelessly.

To make these short-coated dogs even more intriguing, the texture of their coats, or a dash of brown in the colouring, can add to or subtract from their characteristics. Softer-coated dogs can often be more timid than the coarser-coated

The yellow eye is a softer eye. Combined with a longer coat and semi-erect ears, the dog will not be as protective of his space and usually has a more outgoing temperament than the amber-eyed, short-coated Collie.

FIGHT OR FLIGHT DISTANCE

Fight or Flight is the distance between prey and predator that allows a choice. Outside the fight or flight distance the prey has both time and space in its favour to decide how to react – at this point it can take flight. Once the predator reaches the edge of the fight or flight distance, the tension mounts and the choices become limited. If the predator continues to approach, the choice of flight for the prey is lost and the only remaining option is to fight. Because Border Collies with a strong amber eye are capable of almost hypnotizing a sheep with their gaze, their fight or flight distance is greater than that of a darker-eyed collie, which is why, if they are not confident with their handler, they will often react badly to a stranger walking directly into their space.

The shorter-coated dog with a darker eye is more inclined to be nervous, almost to the point of being submissive. Note the tail tucked slightly underneath. They are very sensitive dogs but can soon become over-excitable.

ones, while a dash of tri-colour can dilute some of the tendency for nerves in a submissive dog, but can also heighten the stubbornness in the lighter-eyed dog.

The longer-coated Collie

The dogs with slightly longer coats are no more or less intelligent than their shorter-coated cousins, but they can often be a little more forgiving, thus providing their guardians with a second chance should they make a mistake. The longer-coated, tri-coloured dog with an amber eye may not be quite as challenging as his short-coated equivalent, but he is likely to be more stubborn and, although he may forgive his guardian, he is much less likely to forget or forgive someone who is not a family member and who steps into his designated space. The black and white longer-coated dog with a hazel eye and pricked ears is less prone to making an issue of things that upset him but he is likely to have high energy levels, more so than his Collie cousin with a darker eye and ears that flop over rather than prick up.

A rough coated Border Collie with mottled markings, one blue and one brown eye, and pricked-up ears: beautifully balanced genes, with all the attributes of an energetic and brave dog but sensitive and with a kind nature.

The black and white and tri-coloured dogs are the breed's main foundation colours, but red and blue merles, brown, white, and dogs with mottled faces and legs are also in the genetic mix. Colour genes and character pass down the breed line, which is why the breeding of Border Collies is not only fascinating but highly specialized if the balance of a good temperament with a working mind and body is to be achieved. Equally, purchasing a puppy bred from black and white parents with long coats doesn't guarantee that he will have the long-coated black and white characteristics: the genes from a short-coated, tri-coloured grandparent can carry down the line, missing a generation but featuring strongly in the puppy's character.

White Collies and merle Collies

White Border Collies are often considered to be unpopular for sheepwork for they don't have the ability to slip in quietly behind a flock of sheep as easily their darker-coloured cousins. This may be so in sheepdog trial competitions, but on the hills they used to be considered an asset because they were easily seen by the shepherd when working at dusk.

Blue and red merles have never been prolific in the sheepdog working world as the merle gene, if not bred correctly, is known to cause a number of health problems, mostly deafness and blindness. Although these problems are unusual in a merle to non-merle mating, shepherds who bred for work ability and not appearance would rarely risk bringing a possible problem gene into their line. However, never to cast out the possibility of a working genius, any shepherd with a merle would breed very carefully to make sure it didn't affect his line. Two merles should never be bred together as this results in some double merle puppies, which will inherit the serious health problems carried by the merle gene. Merles from a working line with a strong working instinct are often high energy dogs and they are often so busy being busy that they completely miss what they are being asked to do. A 'wall-eye' is also a characteristic of the merle gene; this is a striking blue eye instead of the usual brown or hazel, and can be one or both eyes. The wall-eye is not

ABOVE: A red-coated, fine-boned dog with semi-erect ears, usually full of life and very excitable.

RIGHT: A much heavier-boned dog with a brown coat and dropped ears: usually has a very placid and easy-going nature but is inclined to be stubborn.

Blue merles are often busy dogs with even temperaments but they can be very excitable. Merles often have one or two blue eyes.

THE INTERNATIONAL SHEEP DOG SOCIETY

The International Sheep Dog Society (ISDS) was formed in 1906 and its Stud Book was set up in the late 1940s. The Stud Books trace back to list 3,000 dogs registered up to 1939, with dates of birth stretching back to the 1890s (where known). The registered dogs are not all the same colour, shape or size; the ability to be able to do the job they were bred for is the main criterion. Three-quarters of a century after the formation of the ISDS the Kennel Club officially recognized the Border Collie as a breed, setting a precedent for a more stereotyped appearance than the huge variety seen in the breed as a working dog. For several years following the Border Collie's initiation into the Kennel Club's breed register the stereotype black and white long-coated dogs were the most popular in pet homes. But a century after the advent of the International Sheep Dog Society the Border Collie had become so popular that every shape, size and colour can be found in companion homes and in the disciplines but, for all the breed may have come a long way in just one century, the Border Collie still remains true to the character of his ancestral genes.

detrimental and is not an indication of defective eyesight. The colour and appearance of a dog's eyes can tell a lot about his character, but two very blue eyes give away little information. A very dark merle dog will usually have standard-coloured eyes but lighter-coloured merles usually have at least one wall-eye, as will Collies with a different-coloured coat if they carry the merle gene.

The importance of understanding breed lines, their traits and characteristics for at least seven generations cannot be stressed enough, not just for the names of dogs that may have excelled in one or more fields of expertise but for the temperament and sensitivity of the chosen line.

Where Border Collies are concerned there is always an element of that wonderful free spirit of theirs proving the exception to any rules, but with the right genes even the exceptions will remain true to the breed's good nature. Sally was a short-coated, prick-eared, tri-coloured Collie with a little bit of mottle and two ice-blue eyes. She was so much of a mixture that all the various characteristics seemed to cancel each other out, and she was a really laid-back little dog who preferred to sit in a deckchair and watch her team-mates work while she received admiring cuddles from passers-by. Similarly there will always be

a long-coated collie with flipped-over ears and dark brown eyes whose character isn't as calm as his appearance may suggest; an investigation into his lineage would probably turn up a few short-coated, prick-eared ancestors in his background, and maybe a little dash of tri-colour as well.

Border Collies are very different in their appearance and in their character, but they are one big happy family of dogs. The path to making them easy to understand, and for training to be a pleasure, is to be sympathetic to the different needs of each one. If you haven't yet found the Border Collie you are going to share your life with, the different dogs mentioned in this chapter will give you an insight into which character is best suited to you and your lifestyle. If you already have a Border Collie in your life, do you recognize the traits? Is he a short-coated dog who likes his space, or a long-coated dog with an abundance of energy, or maybe a long-coated dog with short-coated parents? We will be meeting the dogs mentioned in this chapter again, finding out how different scenarios can affect each one of them and how understanding and managing their different needs will help in teaching them to be well-mannered companions while still retaining their wonderful free spirit.

Rocky's genes carry merle, tri-colour, short coat, blue flecked eyes and sharp ears. Although he was well bred, the breed lines proved incompatible and produced a fiery dog with a dominant nature, requiring careful management.

Tess's genes carry tri-colour, semi-erect ears and a blue eye, but her breed lines were checked carefully for compatibility. She is sensitive, full of fun and loves to learn. Whatever the colour or characteristics of a Border Collie, the attribute that should always be treasured most is their wonderful free spirit.

A SIMPLE BEAUTY

The Border Collie is the epitome of all we may ever desire in a dog, a friend and a partner. Honesty, integrity and loyalty are second nature to a collie and they will work until they can go no further. Yet for all their willingness to give they are not submissive, they are proud of their heritage and they do not suffer fools gladly. Look beyond the colour of the coat and the cloak they wear labelled 'dog', search inside and reach its soul, for once there you will be trapped in a world of unbelievable love and honesty. You will have found true beauty, for the wonderful qualities within this breed are always there waiting to be unlocked and are what make it truly beautiful. Drink in its grace, speed and stamina, for rarely has so much come together so perfectly in so small a package.

2 EXPECTATIONS

Having a preconceived idea of how a puppy (or rescue dog) should behave can often lead to stress, both for the dog and for his guardian. A puppy coming into a new home, where there has previously been a wonderful old dog, cannot be expected to live up to the old dog's reputation. It is easy to forget what the older dog was like as a puppy and just as each human being is different, so is each dog. The new puppy will forge his own niche in his guardian's heart if he is allowed to be himself, and is not constantly compared to a dog that may have been from a different gene line and of a completely different character. As a puppy matures, he learns from the people in his life in ways that may add to his character, and even cause him to develop certain habits. A young puppy coming into a home may develop similar habits and characteristics to the old dog, but it doesn't happen overnight and it may not happen at all; even so, he can be just as loving and as amusing as his predecessor but in his own way. Each dog needs time to develop his own character and, although a puppy needs training and must learn to understand his boundaries, he also needs to have the freedom of choice to grow into his own personality. A child who is constantly told they should be like a particular family member can often grow up to be confused, and if they are really nothing like the aunt or uncle they have been compared to then their own personality can become suppressed. In much the same way, we need to educate and manage any undesirable traits in the puppy, but also encourage him to develop his own individuality.

YOUNG DOGS NEED TIME AND PATIENCE

Hope was tri-coloured with softly pricked ears and a medium coat, and he came from a strong working line. He lived to be fifteen years old and as a youngster was a very strong-willed dog with a dominant nature. He worked sheep and lived in the house and, as he grew older, he found his way into the bedroom and on to the bed. Training Hope as a puppy and as a young dog was challenging as he was both wilful and stubborn, but as he matured he became one of the most gentle and loyal companions anyone could wish for. With a lovely mature dog it's easy to forget the amount of time and patience given to creating the relationship that made that dog so special.

Hope was a challenging youngster with a strong character but he grew to be a most wonderful and gentle old man who taught me so much.

When searching for a new dog or puppy most people know how they would like their dog to look, and sometimes they may have a preconceived idea of how they expect him to behave. But even if someone finds exactly what they have dreamed of, a dog that looks and behaves as expected, it may also be possible that the dog isn't really how they had imagined. Someone who has never had a dog before might base their expectations on a friend's dog and, on finding what they believe to be just the right companion for them, proceed to take advice from their friend. But, as we discovered in the previous chapter, even if the two dogs look alike, it doesn't necessarily follow that they will have similar characters, nor will they necessarily benefit from the same kind of guidance.

BEING FLEXIBLE

A long-coated black and white dog with classic markings may be just what a potential guardian is searching for, and if he comes across such a puppy with an apparently calm temperament he might believe he has found his dream dog. But if the puppy's parents were short-coated or tri-coloured, he may have more energy than anticipated, and if his eyes are amber, he may not welcome the attention of strangers.

In the home it is better to have a flexible rather than a fixed idea of how a dog should behave. A very nervous dog may not feel comfortable with visitors, especially if he is a rescue dog, while a very extrovert dog can be so outgoing that he upsets both visitors and members of the family

A black and white Border Collie but with a slight fleck of tan and pricked ears. If one of her parents had a short coat and amber eyes, her character could lean more to that parent than to her other ancestors.

Ben and Mac are litter brothers. Ben (on the left) is mottled with just a fleck of tan and one blue eye. Mac has more tan, a slightly shorter coat and two blue eyes. Ben had a happy-go-lucky nature but Mac was very sensitive and nervous and had to be managed differently to help him to mature into a confident dog.

alike. These two examples illustrate the dogs' entirely different natures, and if they are handled in the same way the outcome for one of them may not be favourable. However, by giving careful consideration to their different natures, an end result can be achieved of two well-behaved dogs; although one may be more sociable than the other, it need not cause a problem.

It can be disappointing for someone who has set their heart on having a very sociable dog to find their dog is anti-social. They may have envisaged a dog they can take on holiday, that loves camping, enjoys dog shows and long walks with other dogs. However, not all dogs are happy with such scenarios; some may prefer a quiet life at home and may even hide from visitors. But the clues in the previous chapter will help in choosing a puppy, adult or rescue dog to suit the guardian's lifestyle, and also in identifying

why such problems may be present in an existing dog. With understanding and compassion, the reluctant 'happy camper' dog can be made to feel more confident and secure, and, although he may never be over-enthusiastic, patient training may persuade him to do some of the things his guardian had dreamed of sharing with him. However, we can't expect a dog to be happy if he is constantly asked to do something that makes him uncomfortable. If careful training makes a dog feel more confident, but he still doesn't want to join in with his guardian's plans for their future together, then it may be time for a change of direction. Settling for a confident dog who feels secure on local walks and occasional trips away, rather than a dog who is unhappy at being taken into situations he isn't comfortable with, may mean a few unrealized dreams but this will be more than compensated for by the

Puppies and young dogs can be irresistible but they will test the boundaries and need a lot of patience as mistakes made in the first few months can cause habits that can take a long time to correct.

relationship gained with a happy and trusting dog.

Having a puppy should provide the advantage of starting at the beginning with no previous history or issues other than an energetic young dog who will want to test the boundaries. But a potential disadvantage is the temptation to rush and to do too much too soon, and mistakes made in the first few months of a young dog's life may take some rectifying. A rescue or older dog will probably have issues inherited from his past, but they will usually be evident enough to provide an insight into any possible future problems. Quite often potential guardians will visit a rescue centre with a set idea of what they want, and they may even have viewed photographs of a prospective dog, but when introduced to him there may be a slight shadow of doubt that isn't there when they see another dog that is completely different. The dog that tugs at the heartstrings is the one they take home; he is the one they cannot imagine life without and is the one they will change their expectations for.

UNDERSTANDING THE BALANCE

Border Collies do not have to be doing something all the time. No one should be made to feel they are not giving their dog a good home or a good life if they are not 'doing' something with him. In Chapter 1 we discovered just how versatile Border Collies are, both in their characters and in their energy levels, but they are also the masters of 'downtime' if they are allowed to be calm. They are fun-loving, hard-working dogs and they need physical exercise and mental stimulation, but too much of either can create more problems than they solve, so a balance between the two is essential. If a person is very active, either jogging or walking for miles on a regular basis, then a Collie may be the perfect companion, but the more exercise they are given, the more they will expect, as their stamina levels increase. However, a Border Collie can be just as happy with less strenuous exercise, providing this is balanced with an abundance of quality time with his guardian or within the family unit.

Getting the balance into perspective is not only one of the most important factors in keeping a Border Collie both mentally and physically agile, but it is also a vital key to simplifying their training. A Border Collie may be physically tired after a lot of running about, or energetic ball-throwing exercises, and be willing to return home and rest, but the exercise alone is not enough. He also needs quality time with his family to be able

Border Collies are the masters of 'downtime' but if they are always kept on the go they will forget how to switch off. Quiet and calm quality time with your dog is an essential part of forming a bond between you.

LEARNING TO SWITCH OFF

It is essential for a Border Collie training for sheepwork to learn how to switch off. When he has gathered the sheep in, he may have to sit for a long time waiting patiently for the shepherd to vaccinate or worm his flock. He may be called to move the flock forward into the pen and he will be expected to keep an eye on the sheep, but part of his training will include having the self-control to stand back when asked to.

Kim was taken to the sheep every day for training but she soon began to escape from the yard and go to the sheep field without permission. Her handler became concerned that she was becoming a workaholic, and a dog who becomes so fixated on working that he won't switch off can be a danger to the flock. After careful thought he kept her away from the sheep for a few days and then began walking around his land so she could see the sheep but was not expected to work them. She soon settled down and learned to switch off when she realized that their 'down time' pleased her handler as much as working did.

Border Collies love company and an old dog wants to wake from his daily nap to see a loving face and to feel a gentle hand stroking him.

Young dogs regularly left on their own can soon get into mischief and two can be double trouble!

to enjoy the companionship and to create the wonderful bond that human and dog can share. Equally the Collie that has a more sedentary life needs the balance of a good walk; it doesn't need to be a fast and furious run around or ball-chasing exercise, but it does need to be a walk that will take the edge off his energy, allowing him to remain a calm and contented dog.

Border Collies need stability, but they don't have to have routine – in fact, once in a routine they can become quite demanding – but consistency is vital for them. They won't sulk or throw a tantrum if their food doesn't materialize at the same time each day, unless they have a strict feeding routine and then woe betide any change

that occurs in that routine, but they do need to know that they will be fed each day. They need some form of exercise every day but it doesn't have to be at the same time, or for the same length of time, or for the same distance. Just as we may hope that they will live up to some of our dreams, they too have their own expectations. They love company and if they have one or two weeks of company and time spent with them, they can't understand why they are suddenly left alone when everyone in the home has gone back to work and to school. The consistency and the company have gone and from having fun and plenty of exercise they are left alone, so before long a young dog will begin to amuse himself and get into mischief. Not having a strict routine allows for some changes in day-to-day patterns, but Border Collies love companionship and do not cope with being left alone for long and regular periods of time.

TIME TO LEARN

One of the wonderful qualities dogs are blessed with, and that we humans often struggle with, is being content with the present. A dog's recognition of the past is by a memory flash, be it an incident, a smell or a person, and they know

SHEPHERD'S COMMENT:

'Show me a dog that is in full work at one year old and I'll struggle to find him when he's seven. Show me a dog that has been allowed his youth and to develop at his own pace and I will have a job to stop him working when he's reached retirement!'

Collies learn things quickly but they can also pick up bad habits just as quickly. A simple Border Collie 'task' of digging for a bug or a worm can soon turn into a massive excavation.

nothing of tomorrow, whereas we can bring back our yesterdays at will, and are constantly thinking about and planning our tomorrows. We have to think about tomorrow because we are the organizers of our own and our dogs' lives, and without forward planning our lives would be chaotic. However, as good as we are at planning ahead to what we want to do and how we intend to achieve it, we are sometimes in danger of trying to achieve it too quickly.

Because Border Collies are intelligent and always willing and eager to learn, people are often misled into thinking they are easy to train. Indeed, they are easy if they receive information they understand, but just as they are quick to learn what we want them to do, they are equally quick at picking up bad habits and there is a risk of trying to teach them too much too soon. With this comes the same risk as in the Shepherd's Comment: dogs that learn to sit, down, stay, give a paw, retrieve, plus countless other commands can be so full of information, and have been almost pushed into maturity, that at

some point they may revert back to the 'naughty puppy' stage. When this happens in an adult dog it can lead to the development of behavioural problems. Collies need time to grow and time to learn, and if each new piece of information we teach them is followed too quickly by another one, they can soon become overloaded. This may result in them 'forgetting' some very simple and basic commands, and becoming frustrated as their handler perseveres in trying to move their training a stage forward. Quite often a young dog will appear to have completely forgotten something that only a few days previously he not only understood but enjoyed doing. A young dog in training rarely forgets something he has been taught, but if he has had too much information loaded onto him he may temporarily 'store' what he already knows while he processes the new information. A dog being trained to work sheep can have mastered how to gather a small flock, bring it to his handler and go left and right when told. However, when he is given something new to learn, for example how to drive the sheep away again, he may struggle for a while to do both, until he stores what he has learned and concentrates on mastering the new information. An impatient shepherd can jeopardize his relationship with his dog if he is not sympathetic to the problem; he must understand that everything he has taught his dog is still there, but he must be patient and wait until the dog feels confident enough to bring out of his memory-store all that he learned previously. The shepherd may be hoping for a dog that can be trained to do all aspects of sheepwork but his hopes and expectations can soon be dashed if he doesn't put patience before pressure. There is little difference between training a dog to work

Whatever hopes and dreams you may have for your dog and his future, little can compare to seeing the joy and love on your dog's face as he runs to be with you.

sheep or any other form of training when it comes to impatience and pressure. A young dog under pressure will make mistakes and pressure on a dog is usually caused by an impatient handler.

The most important thing when choosing a dog to share your life is being able to bond with him and to create a relationship. There is nothing wrong with having dreams, but if the dog cannot do what is expected of him then they may have to remain just dreams. The dog you have may never be what you thought he could be, and may not be able to do all the things you hoped he would, but he will still be the dog you love. You just need to learn to travel a different path together.

FOR THE LOVE OF YOU

I have two ears that listen to all you say
I have two eyes that watch every move
 you make
I have a heart and a soul that I give to
 you
I am a dog and I give without question
I will live and I will die for you
I ask for one thing in return
I ask for you.

3 WELCOME HOME

Border Collies are hardy souls and many a young working dog, at the end of a long day, has turned down a cosy comfortable straw bed in a warm barn in favour of an extra hour outside in a wet and windy yard. No matter how tired or how wet, the desire to be near his shepherd, not to miss anything and to be ready and able to work again at the drop of a hat, is far greater than the draw of the warm bed.

The lifestyle that many Border Collies lead today may be very different from that of a working dog, but the willingness to please and to serve are still there. They were referred to as a working companion by the shepherds, who spent every waking moment working with them and recognized and nurtured the companionship they had to offer. As working dogs they should not be denied company or companionship, and as domestic companions they should not be denied the recognition of their heritage and their natu-ral instincts, for it is the qualities that make them masters in their working environment that we are drawn to and love about them.

The Border Collie you take into your home may be only very distantly related to those dogs of yesteryear, working from dawn till dusk with shepherds who, before the advent of tractors and quad bikes, had to rely on a stout pair of boots to make travelling easier. But modern-day farmers and shepherds on the steep fells and vast moorlands still need dependable sheepdogs to gather their flocks, and although farming may have changed, Border Collies and their ability to work have not. They are still the same dogs carrying the same genes and, although a companion dog may not be working for a living, and has a soft warm bed instead of a bale of straw to sleep on, knowing more about his past can help us to understand some of the simple needs of our modern-day Border Collie.

A Collie will take time to rest at the end of a long hard day but will always be ready to go again at the drop of a hat.

REST AND RELAXATION

In addition to knowing how a collie works, it helps to understand how they relax and what makes them feel safe. Dogs love to play but they have their own idea about games; in a group they will play their version of tag, on their own they will find something that amuses them and will be happy to play with it alone without any input from another dog or a person. They love to roll, though their choice of what to roll in may seem strange to us. But long grass is cooling and relaxing, while on a rougher surface wriggling around on their backs must be heaven for them, like a massage and a good scratch all rolled into one, and if they can find something smelly they are happy to cover themselves in it. When it comes to sleeping, their basic instincts tell them to make sure they are protecting themselves, so they will curl up in the smallest space possible. A hole they have dug, a box they have found, or a small enclosure – all offer safety and security where they can see everything that is approaching, but nothing can get at them from behind.

Border Collies know how to amuse themselves when they have time off. Despite the weather and the mud, three generations are thoroughly enjoying themselves taking time out to watch the 'duck show'.

NATURAL PROTECTION

At five weeks old Meg's litter of pups loved to follow their mum around the garden but, during a rainstorm, the door blew shut and Meg couldn't get back inside. Her guardian was panic-stricken when the puppies couldn't be found – but when the rain stopped Meg and her brood reappeared on the lawn playing. All the puppies were warm and dry. Meg had taken them to a very overgrown part of the garden and dug a hole just big enough for them all to fit in; there they had snuggled up together, warm, dry and happy. Not being indoors was no problem for Meg: her natural instincts had told her how to look after her family and how to keep them safe and protect them.

A PUPPY IN THE HOME

The great thing about dogs is how simple their lives are: they eat, drink, play and relax, and when they have food and drink supplied for them, without the need to hunt, then life becomes even simpler for them. With this in mind, taking a new puppy into the home shouldn't prove difficult, but no matter how easy it may seem to begin with, questions soon begin to arise: what type of bed, how many different kinds of lead, which collar is best, how many toys to provide,

A shy or nervous puppy will love a place of his own where he can feel snug and safe.

and which to choose out of all the different kinds of dog food? Suddenly life has begun to be difficult and the puppy hasn't arrived yet! We can learn so much from how dogs live naturally that bringing up a puppy doesn't need to be complicated, as long as he or she understands who the parent or pack leader in the family is, and the rules and boundaries are consistent.

A puppy will love a place of his own, some- where he can feel safe and protected, and not too big because he wants to feel secure; if it's in a nice quiet part of the home, he will be able to settle down and rest without being disturbed. Every dog and every circumstance is different, and a nervous puppy needs to be managed differently from a more boisterous one. Whereas the shy or nervous puppy needs his own space to feel safe in, a more forward or dominant puppy

A very confident or bold puppy needs a place of his own for some time out to keep calm.

will benefit from having a 'time out' area of his own.

A house crate

Not everyone likes the idea of a crate; mentally the words 'crate' or 'cage' conjure up something that restricts freedom and is unkind. It is not right to leave a dog in one for hours on end, but thinking of it as a dog's personal bedroom or 'Dog Den' can bring a whole new perspective to the 'house crate'. A child's bedroom is somewhere to retreat to, a safe haven and a place to escape from visitors. As adults, the bedroom is often the one place we crave to be when under pressure – a place where we can be ourselves, have some time out and recover our strength. A puppy needs to be made to feel just as secure as a small child, and a crate can become his bedroom, his own space where he can rest and escape from any noise or from visitors he is unsure of – his own Dog Den. This Den can soon become the

dog's best friend, his own bit of home that is comforting and familiar when travelling in a car, when you are visiting friends and family or going on holiday.

But a crate can soon be transformed into the puppy or dog's own Dog Den, his own personal space, and can be made really cosy.

Not everyone likes the idea of a house crate and it can seem a little bleak.

This photograph wasn't planned but Tweed, one of our rescue dogs, invaded the photo shoot and decided it was just too good a Den to be missed and moved in!

NIGHT-TIME TIP

If a puppy doesn't have his own space, he has no security or boundaries. His mother would have made a bed for her puppies to nestle into, and once snuggled up to her at night he would have felt safe, but in a strange house with no defined safe area he will feel insecure. Given a Dog Den with lovely warm bedding to burrow into, and something familiar to snuggle up to, he will soon settle. If he doesn't, try to resist the urge to take him into your bedroom to sleep with you, as you may find it difficult to break the habit and he will soon be a big adolescent dog who may refuse to let you out of his sight. Instead, go to him and sit with him whilst he is still in his Den; put some soft music on and be prepared to stay with him until he settles. This way he will learn that he is safe and that you are never far away but he will also understand that bedtime is a time for settling down. If you want your dog in your bedroom, there will be plenty of time to take him there later, once the boundaries have been established.

For a puppy to feel he has his own space, the Dog Den needs to be somewhere peaceful; suggested areas are a quiet corner of a living room, a not-too-busy kitchen, or a utility room or cloakroom (providing they are not cold). Each choice comes with advantages and disadvantages. A Dog Den in a living room does mean a puppy can be observed, but if it's a busy room he may find it difficult to settle and, although it's his own space, it is in the middle of everyone else's activity. A quiet area in a room that is not the centre of family activity is better, but once he has rested, he won't want to be left alone for any length of time.

House-training
A Dog Den can offer a huge advantage when it comes to house-training. The easier we make it for puppies to understand what we want of them, the quicker they learn. Dogs rarely soil their own bed area, and puppies need to toilet far more often than adult dogs, usually after waking from a deep sleep and very soon after a meal. If the Den door is closed when the puppy is asleep, he won't be able to wake up and wander straight out into the room and perform his motions in the first convenient spot. If there is some paper in his Den he has the option to use it as a toilet area, but most puppies, if they know they are going to be let out, soon learn to hang on a little longer. Once outside, they can be taken to a designated area and given plenty of praise for being such a clean puppy. This method also helps to establish some boundaries as the puppy doesn't have immediate access to any part of the home. Access is granted when the Den door is opened. This may seem like a minor boundary but if the puppy has a strong or forceful character, which probably won't be revealed for several weeks, it will help to keep him calm and to establish some early training.

Other beds and bedding
A Dog Den is the equivalent of a dog's bedroom but he also needs his own space in other areas of the home. There is a variety of beds and bedding to choose from, but remember that puppies love to chew, so giving one a really soft bouncy bed or a bean bag may tempt him to find out what's inside it. There are some excellent solid beds, and soft bedding can be used as a mattress. Even if the soft bedding needs to be removed because the puppy is chewing, the solid bed that has his own scent on it is still there as a constant in his life. Because a dog's bed needs to be a safe place, it must be situated where it can remain, at least until the puppy has settled in. Constantly moving it because it's in the way of visitors, the television or the children's play area can not only confuse a puppy when he goes to his Den and it's not

Mossie has her own Dog Den but also a bed in the living room. As a 'teenager', she loves to sit and play roller ball. As a puppy grows up, his bed should always be his happy place.

there, but, worse, can also make him feel insecure. So when choosing a bed make sure it will fit into the area you have in mind for it. It doesn't have to be huge as we have already learned that puppies love to curl up and feel safe, so rather than buying a very big bed which has to be filled with lots of bedding, getting a smaller bed with cosy bedding could prove a much better option both for the puppy and in terms of house space.

SAFETY FIRST

When you bring a puppy into your life, you want him to be happy and safe, and somewhere in the back of your mind you have an image of the dream dog you want him to be when he grows up. In some ways dogs see the world very differently from us: they don't think about yesterday or worry about tomorrow; they don't crave creature comforts; and they are actually happy with a very simple diet. Yet in other ways dogs and humans have a lot in common: dogs understand the family unit, as part of their pack heritage; and they understand respect for elders and firm sensible rules for younger members, since in the wild adhering to rules and boundaries helps to keep them safe. The main difference between the pack dog and the domestic or working dog is the provision of food and safety. Domestic dogs are given a permanent 'pack' area, which gives them protection, and they don't need to hunt for each meal as it is provided for them. The latter is not difficult for us to understand and adhere to; we know that our dogs need feeding every day and, apart from deciding which type of food to give, it's a very easy part of looking after a dog. But we often don't realize how important safety is for them. We discourage them from any form of self-protection, we don't want them to fight other dogs, we want them to get on with children, and we don't want them to take matters into their own paws if they decide they don't like the family's non-favourite uncle or aunt. For the family to argue with a relative may be acceptable but we can't have our dogs nipping at their heels just because they don't find them agreeable – but what if they find someone a little threatening? They are in the home they are supposed to be safe in, and a person who makes them feel unsafe is trying to stroke them – and their protectors, the family, aren't doing anything to prevent it.

LOSING CONFIDENCE

Jess was a very happy and confident puppy when she went into her new home; her proud guardians let everyone cuddle her and she loved all the attention. But in the first two weeks Jess was frightened by one of the visitors, a family member with a loud voice, who kept staring at her and trying to pick her up. The family were upset that she was not accepting this man and, forgetting that he was actually a stranger to her, they picked her up and placed her on his knee. He was happy to have her to cuddle for a few moments, but in those few moments the relationship between Jess and her guardians changed and she went from being a confident puppy to being nervous and feeling vulnerable. It was a long time before she felt she could trust her guardians again and her months of puppyhood, which should have been fun for her and her family, became months of building bridges and regaining Jess's trust.

Jess was introduced to everyone as a puppy, but she lost her confidence.

GAINING CONFIDENCE

Megan didn't leave the farm until she was a year old. She had been introduced to very few people and she had never been in a position where she felt threatened or unsafe. At one year old she attended a sheepdog demonstration and was more than happy to meet and greet with the large audience, even though she wasn't used to seeing so many people. Because Megan had always felt safe and protected, she had grown into a confident outgoing dog.

Megan didn't meet many people as a puppy yet she grew into a confident young dog.

There are no strict rules for bringing up a puppy as they are all very different but it should be remembered that prevention is always better than cure. To keep things in perspective, it often helps to draw a parallel between puppies and young children. Children need to feel they can trust their parents, but that trust can be severely compromised if the parents put them in a position which makes them feel threatened. However, whereas a child can understand the words of a promise that all will be well, a puppy has to rely on tone of voice and trust, both of which take time to establish. There are countless puppies who have been introduced to a lot of people and taken into many different scenarios and have grown up to be confident adult dogs. There are also many who have felt vulnerable at some time but have learned how to manage uncomfortable situations so well on their own that they appear not to have any issues. To establish a really good bond of love and trust with a puppy is the most important aspect to the start of training, with slow and sure progress being preferable to rushing and putting that relationship at risk. For the first few days it is better to keep visitors to a minimum so the puppy can settle down and has a chance to establish who is a permanent part of his life and who he can turn to in times of trouble.

PUPPY FOOD

There are many different kinds of dog food available and for first-time dog owners it can be very confusing, especially as dog food manufacturers cannot cater for all breeds and sizes in the feeding guides given on their products. A good complete food should contain all the vitamins and minerals needed, as can home-made food, but it can be more difficult to balance home-made meals, and an unbalanced diet can result in a puppy either lacking in some important nutrients, or receiving an excess of energy-producing ingredients.

Whether feeding a complete food or giving a home-made diet of meat and biscuits, it's impor-

TIP: THE GOLDEN SEVEN

The first seven months of a dog's life is one of the most important times for building a foundation of love and trust, and what happens in those months can stay with the dog throughout his life. A young dog neglected or abused may be very nervous or may turn to aggression for protection; placed in a loving home he can learn to trust again, but those first seven months will have defined how he reacts to certain situations, and his new guardian will need to learn how to manage those situations in order to gain his trust. A young dog in a loving home, who is frightened by something such as his first trip in a car or a passing motorbike, will carry that memory through his life but with a bond of love and trust he will turn to his guardian for safety, minimizing the risk of future problems.

A young dog enjoying himself. His body is turning on an angle but he is relaxed and balanced. Collies are very supple but if they become over-excited their bodies cease to be as relaxed.

An older dog with all four legs off the ground. His far side rear leg will touch down first and take all his weight. Correct diet and exercise in a young dog are an essential part of keeping the joints strong and supple.

intake can speed up a dog's rate of growth), the young dog's growth has slowed down, probably just adding another inch or so and filling out; at this point the dog's energy intake needs to be reduced to a good adult diet. Although this may sound confusing, it can be boiled down to monitoring the puppy's growth and energy levels. It doesn't make sense to feed the same energy food to a young dog through all his growth periods, so as the growth rate slows down the diet needs to be adjusted accordingly. This helps to prevent pushing the dog's body into a growth rate that is too fast, and it also helps to manage energy levels, as feeding a young dog in excess of his requirements can cause, or exacerbate, existing problems and may also lead to hyperactivity.

BUILDING A FOUNDATION

Mistakes are inevitable when bringing up and training a dog but with a good foundation of basic training most can easily be rectified. It may seem harmless fun when a puppy runs around the house from room to room, but will it be as amusing when he is a big boisterous dog? It might not give too much cause for concern if he chews his toys, but will you be happy when he's taking shoes from the hall and clothes from the radiator to chew?

tant to feed according to the puppy's growth rate and to know when to change the energy levels in the food. There are three main growth phases. In the first few weeks of a puppy's life he will practically triple in size, which means he is using a lot of energy and therefore needs a diet high in good nutritional energy. Most of this first growth spurt takes place before, during and immediately after weaning, so the first phase of growth is well established by the time the puppy goes into his new home.

In the puppy's second growth phase he will probably double in height. This requires less energy than the first phase, and therefore the puppy doesn't need the same amount of energy intake. In the third growing phase, which in a Border Collie is usually from six months (the age may vary according to the energy input given in the previous growth periods, as a high-energy

The Dog Den is an ideal starting point for building a good foundation for later training. The Den is the puppy's own space, his private bedroom; it is his to sleep, play and be safe in. This area is his and just as you will respect his space and not invade it or take his things, so he will learn to respect your space. Understanding the natural instincts of a dog makes communication easier and, although a puppy will always test the boundaries, he will expect to have parental guidance as to what those boundaries are. In the wild a puppy must learn manners before going into the adolescent pack; if not, he can become defiant and a rebel in the group constitutes a danger to the entire pack. It is the equivalent of the disruption caused in a family by a defiant child lacking in good manners and parental respect.

SIMPLE BOUNDARIES

It is important not to overload a puppy with too much information, especially in the first few weeks when all he really needs is to feel warm and loved and to know that he has a protector. Making a puppy feel loved isn't difficult but being a parent figure isn't always easy: it's very difficult to say 'no' to a cuddly little ball of fluff with huge appealing eyes! In fact most people find it easier to say 'no' to a child. But being just a little firm now and then, and letting the puppy know that there are boundaries to be heeded, also tells him that you are in control, that you are the parent figure or the leader in his little pack. This is what he needs to know, as he is no longer with his canine mum who would have made sure that he did as he was told and had good manners; he would instinctively have known he was safe with her. A puppy in a new home given everything – love, lots of toys, freedom and few restrictions – may be happy enough, but at the first sign of a problem he may still feel isolated.

A puppy always has one eye on his canine mum, as he relies on her for guidance, but he doesn't receive a treat each time he looks at her or does her bidding. It's enough for him to know she is pleased, which she shows by gently licking or nuzzling him, her way of showing affection. Each time your puppy looks at you smile back at him, stop what you are doing and give him a stroke; encourage him to keep up that rapport with you, as this is part of the foundation needed to maintain a good relationship with him when he reaches adolescence, which can be a rebellious time for most dogs. Treats are fine in context, for example when he goes to bed, when he's been exceptionally good or when you feel like treating him, but there is no treat, no matter how tasty, that should be more important than you. Remember, we are tapping into a dog's mind to make communication and training easier; dogs love to love, and while the receiving of a treat is a short-lived pleasure (once eaten it is quickly disregarded), a loving hand and a soft word are never forgotten.

TOYS

Toys can help a puppy to develop by teaching him to think and to work out situations, but they are

ABOVE: *With a little encouragement puppies can be very good at amusing themselves. 'I have a reason to be searching here.'*

LEFT: *Puppies need gentle guidance but don't overload them with information. Keep everything simple and they will enjoy bonding with you.*

'Found it!'

not a substitute for communication or companionship. A toy to keep a dog amused while he is on his own prevents boredom, and a different toy to teach him simple games such as 'which hand is it in?' or 'which cup is it under?' not only teaches the dog to think out the problem but helps to strengthen the relationship between human and dog.

CASE HISTORY – KERRY

Kerry, a rescue dog, was toy- and ball-obsessed. If she saw a ball or a toy she would focus on it and refuse to give her attention back to her handler. Once she had the object of her focus in her possession, she would not give it up and would bite anyone trying to retrieve it from her; she would throw it around becoming almost hysterical as she ran round and round the garden.

For several weeks Kerry lived without a toy, her diet was changed to reduce her hyperactivity and she learned to walk properly on a lead without pulling. As Kerry's mind began to let go of her obsessive ball games, she was introduced to a search dummy; she was only allowed it in the garden and it was never thrown – instead it was just quietly hidden for her to find. She was on a long line and if she started to get excited she was asked to sit down and settle; once calmer she could resume her search. Within two days Kerry learned to stay calm and thoroughly enjoyed looking for her special toy. Kerry's puppyhood had been spent with an abundance of toys and endless ball-throwing exercises, and she had become hyperactive and nippy. During her time in rehabilitation Kerry learned a different and calmer way of playing, and how to communicate with her handler and enjoy their relationship.

TOP RIGHT: *Collies love to love, and their toys should be well down their list of priorities. The look in a dog's eye should be for the person they love and not what that person can throw for them.*

BOTTOM RIGHT: *A dog should not become so toy-obsessed that he refuses to recall from it or becomes destructive.*

AN ADULT DOG IN THE HOME

There are two main differences between taking an adult dog or a puppy into your life: one is age and the other is the memory bank. Some people prefer not to go through the puppy stages of house-training and teething, and the problems often associated with an adolescent dog, but the older dog has already been through this process and will have certain habits and traits stored in his memory bank. For this reason it is better to introduce the older dog into the home just as you would a puppy. By providing a bed in a quiet area and keeping the home as calm as possible you will give him time to observe his new home from the sanctuary of a safe haven. Like us, dogs need time to adjust and to learn about their surroundings and the new people in their lives without any pressure being put on them.

SHEPHERD'S COMMENT:

'If something is going wrong and you're not sure how to put it right, there is no point in persisting. Take time out to figure out how to solve the problem and put your dog back to bed so he can figure out why the fun stopped. Don't rush back into the field and don't get annoyed with your dog; get annoyed with yourself for not understanding him better but don't carry that annoyance back into the field. You'll be surprised how forgiving he is that you're not able to understand him all the time but he'll not be as forgiving if you don't try.'

Time is very important even for a dog with no known history, but all dogs deserve this time out to settle in and to feel safe. Even if you know the dog really well (and in this chapter we are looking at a dog who is familiar to you and not a rescue dog), he may have little habits that you are unaware of, and for a dog in a new home, even with someone he knows, it can be dis-tressing when something he is used to doing or something happening suddenly stops. It may be something really simple that the previous owner didn't think to mention, like a certain routine or a biscuit at bedtime, or it could be something more significant, such as reacting to certain things on the television, or being allowed on the furniture. The bedtime routine is easy to accomplish and it is important as it will help him to feel some familiarity in his new home, but other routines or habits may be something you wish to change, or manage differently from his previous home. If you are forewarned it is much easier, but the need to change things gently is very important.

If a dog is accustomed to sitting on furniture, he will find it difficult to understand if this isn't going to be allowed in his new home. Some dogs do not take offence at being asked to get off the furniture, but to some it can be the one change in their new life that makes them feel insecure. A gentle and kind way of doing this, in a way the dog can understand, is to allow him on one piece of furniture but put a throw (a blanket or fleece) over it, and in the first week make sure he is only on that piece of furniture and only when the throw is on it. If he gets on the furniture and the throw isn't in place, ask him to get off, put the throw on and invite him back up on to the throw, and after a period of time he will begin to associate his place as being on the throw and not on the furniture. If your new dog doesn't do as you ask, have a lead ready to put on him so you can show him what you want; a dog who has been told to 'get off' furniture won't understand a different term such as 'get down', which could mean something entirely different to him. A house lead attached to his collar means you can gently encourage him down from the furniture while you introduce him to his new life and familiarize him with new commands. Never take hold of a dog's collar and pull him to where you want him to be, as this is a direct confrontation to a dog and can make a strong-minded dog want to be dominant and a gentle or sensitive dog may be made to feel submissive, neither of which you want in your dog. There are often things that people don't ask about a dog they are giving a

No matter how cute and cuddly they are as puppies, they grow into adolescent dogs who will push the boundaries.

home to, and things his previous owner may not consider to be important, but the more information you have the easier it will be for the dog to settle in.

SUMMARY

The first few months of a puppy's life are full of fun, learning new things together and lots of cuddles, but at approximately six months old a Border Collie can turn from a dependent puppy into an adolescent dog almost overnight and it will be natural for him to push the boundaries.

METHODS

If he seems too excitable, or becomes defiant and refuses to listen to you, the first item on the check-list is his diet. Make sure he is not being fed energy in excess of his requirements. Protein and fat or oil content give a good indication of energy levels in a food. A useful guide is to feed 27 per cent protein to a puppy, reducing this to 24 per cent as his growth slows down and to 20 per cent in the final growth stage; these levels are in balance with the puppy's three major growth spurts and will help to keep the energy natural and not food-induced. Most dogs on a

43

diet too high in energy will have really shiny coats but are often underweight, and if they are fed extra to encourage weight gain it simply adds more energy to an already overloaded system. Energy also needs to be fed with consideration given to the dog's genetics; most short-coated, prick-eared Collies, for example, have a naturally high energy level. Once the energy level is reduced (and it can take several weeks) the dog will be more settled and is therefore more likely to gain weight and to fill out. Checking the diet also applies to the older dog, who doesn't need his energy levels monitored for growth, but he does need to be on a calming diet for the first few weeks.

At the first sign of problem behaviour with a new puppy or older dog in the home take a step back and provide time out for yourself and for your dog. Then go back to doing something that he is very familiar with, but don't push him – dogs soon get confused if too much information has been made available to them. They also benefit from 'thinking time' – something which the old shepherds found invaluable.

CASE HISTORY – BEN

Ben's owners were emigrating and friends offered him a permanent home with them. He came to them with a bed, a blanket, some food, a few toys and a long list of Ben's 'words'. For the first day he seemed happy; he was being made a fuss of and getting lots of attention, but too many pieces of information were missing from that list. It included how to get him to sit, stay, give a paw, roll over and speak for a titbit, but it didn't include the magic word needed to encourage him to 'go' in the garden, nor did it mention that the word bed was accompanied by a clap of the hands. They weren't to know that Ben was used to running up and down the stairs several times before bed time, and they thought he had gone a little crazy when he did his usual routine. Ben became withdrawn and unhappy, and his new family had to go right back to basics, almost as if he were a puppy, teaching new words to actions as the words which they had been told he knew sounded different to him when coming from someone else. Ben became more and more confused until they provided him with a very quiet area in their home and stopped trying to get him to do anything. When Ben needed something he let them know, and they began to teach him new words for whatever he was asking for. Within a month Ben changed from a lonely and confused dog back to the lovely bouncy lad he was before.

4 KEEPING CALM

Puppies learn behaviour from their mother and older siblings, and in a native, or instinctive, pack environment they are constantly receiving information they understand. Because the pack runs as a tightly knit family they rarely make mistakes and, on the few occasions when they do, there is always a higher-ranking dog in the vicinity to guide the erring youngster back on track. A puppy (or an older dog) living with a human family doesn't receive the same information as in the pack environment. We have more rules and regulations, we ask more of our dogs and we provide less down-time for them, plus we are speaking in a language they have to work hard to understand. An older dog can help with the rearing of a puppy providing he is a calm and sensible dog,

It's lovely for dogs to have company but care needs to be taken to ensure young dogs don't bond so closely together that they ignore their human family.

but to allow a youngster to learn from a dog that has existing training problems, or is simply not mature enough to take on the responsibility of chaperoning a youngster, can result in a puppy taking on all the older dog's behaviour problems, as well as any adolescent ones of his own.

LIVING WITH ANOTHER DOG

Another dog can be good company for a newcomer but, although this may have the benefit of helping a new dog or puppy to settle in, it can also have the disadvantage of taking his attention away from his new family. Dogs speak the same language so they can communicate and play together, and suddenly the guardian ceases to be an important part of the dogs' lives. The dogs become friends, they understand and listen to each other and they become a little team of their own, almost by-passing the people who love and look after them.

Having fun and playing together is fine but, as with children, there comes a time when a parent feels the need to step in and calm the game down. But whereas we can tell children that it's time to stop playing and settle down calmly, it isn't as easy to explain that to a dog. Dogs have to learn our language in order to be able to understand certain words and commands, but while teaching them our language we also need to learn theirs. It's very one-sided to expect a dog to learn all the words we want to teach them without finding out more about their way of communication, which is natural and fun to learn; what's more, with knowledge of how to converse with them, it becomes much easier to train them.

BODY LANGUAGE

The universal language of most animals is body language and dogs are the masters of 'silent' discussions. With simple, barely noticeable movements a dog can have passed an opinion and made a decision based on that judgement without anyone noticing, unless they are tuned in to him and to how a dog thinks. Border Collies have wonderfully supple bodies and when they move they almost seem to flow, which means their communication is gentle and flowing; if they were human, they would have a beautiful,

Border Collies have wonderfully supple bodies and when they run they almost flow across the ground. If their body language were vocal, they would have a gentle, almost magical, flow of words.

almost magical flow of words that commands people to listen. In their native environment they would learn from siblings and senior family members, which means we need to be sympathetic to what they expect of a leader or a parent figure. If we can provide what they are looking for in a way they understand, and that enables them to give us their complete trust, we are creating the foundation for the partnership that earned dogs the title of man's best friend.

Dogs learn a lot from copying and quite often they will become a mirror image of any movement they see regularly. One of the most positive attributes of a Dog Den for a puppy is that he need never be greeted by a distressed or upset guardian. It is difficult to be calm and happy if, after an hour's shopping, you return home to find furniture chewed and soiled carpets, and a puppy will soon pick up on a negative or distressed mood. But, secure in his den, whatever he has done is in his own patch, so he can be greeted with a happy smiling face and a cheerful mood, which means you can both look forward to a happy greeting and a positive atmosphere.

FLASH THE COPYCAT

Flash came into rescue as a food-aggressive dog who had been abused for his aggression. For a long time he had to be fed outside his pen and with nobody near him. Eventually he began to learn that his food wasn't going to be taken from him and he began to relax. His body was no longer stiff and anxious when he was eating and he stopped guarding his food as there was nobody to guard it against. Eventually Flash became so relaxed that he could be fed in his pen – he had come to understand that he would never be hurt and his food never taken from him, but when feeding him I kept my body calm and smiled at him as I put his dish down. But instead of simply smiling each time I fed him, I must have grinned because over a period of weeks Flash began to grin back at me, which was a little disconcerting to begin with, but it soon became a little greeting game we played. I went in with his food and he grinned at me; I grinned back and put his dish down; and he gave me another big grin before tucking into his meal.

Collies are great mimickers, and with gentle body movements Digby became a mirror image; by watching the movement of the feet very carefully and then copying, he began to walk backwards and forwards as if dancing.

THE CALM BODY

When a dog is working sheep he can turn on a sixpence and change direction almost without interrupting the calm flow of body movement, and a fully trained dog knows that any sudden or sharp movements will upset the sheep, causing an adverse reaction. If you watch a dog working sheep, you will notice that he will run to keep

A Collie can convey messages with its body language. Megan is being strong and firm, not shouting at the sheep but making sure they know they have to go where she wants.

When Megan has the sheep doing her bidding, she drops back and her body is almost a whisper.

them moving but if one turns to face him he will stand still, keeping on the edge of the sheep's fight or flight distance until it turns back to the flock, and then he will creep forwards, almost on tiptoe. When he is creeping forwards his language is almost a whisper. But if he is trying to get a flock of reluctant sheep through a gateway his movements will be sharper, with faster turns, and he will work much nearer to them; with his body language he is shouting at them to get them moving. This information gives us a valuable insight into a dog's mind and can help us to understand how some of our actions can affect them. If we move quickly, with sharp actions, we are communicating at a much higher volume with our bodies than if we remain calm and flowing with our movements. Sheep will remain calm when the dog is calm but in response to his sudden and sharp movements they become anxious; likewise, a dog can soon become stressed or lose confidence if doesn't understand a person's body language or intentions.

THE MIRROR IMAGE

Because dogs understand body language they rely on what they see as well as on what they hear, so a soft voice combined with harsh or sharp body movements can give out mixed and confusing messages. Dogs learn by observation and the way a person acts and moves can either provoke a dog to behave erratically or encourage him to be calm, as he will become a mirror image of that person's behaviour and movements. However, whereas a calm and flowing body movement gives a clear signal of gentleness and strength to a dog, which will help him to feel safe and able to relax, an adverse reaction can be caused by a strong or erratic body language, which can make a strong dog react in a similar manner and show signs of aggression, while a nervous dog may feel intimidated. Equally, someone who moves cautiously around their dog and is a little indecisive can also create mirror images: the nervous or shy dog will feel he doesn't have a leader or parent figure, and the stronger dog will see an opportunity to take advantage and may become dominant in order to get his own way.

PAUSE AND THINK

Whenever you are unsure of how to deal with a situation, Pause and Think (PAT). Stand back and take some deep breaths before committing to an action that could make matters worse, and upset your dog and the relationship you have with him. To come home to a soiled carpet and chewed-up garments taken from the radiator, or a pair of shoes half-eaten and a chair leg nibbled at may not be pleasant, and will probably make your body language send messages to your dog that will tell him you are not pleased. But take a step back. The carpet will clean, the chewed-up garments and shoes can be replaced and the chair leg repaired. Think first about how it happened: why was he able to do those things when being in a Dog Den, or his own area, could have prevented it, and if it's the first time he's done it you can prevent it from happening again by providing a safe area for him. Take some deep breaths, remove your dog to his own area or Den, then start the cleaning-up process; while you are doing that your dog will be taking time out on his own to think about why the fun has stopped and why you didn't want to join in.

What you are thinking

You have come home to a mess and you're not sure why your dog has done it; the socks were on the radiator, he's been told not to carry shoes around and what was he thinking when he soiled the carpet and chewed the chair? Maybe he's never done anything like it before, in which case you are probably wondering what he is going to do next, and if he has done it before you perhaps thought that after making it quite clear you were not happy last time he would never do it again.

What your dog is thinking

He's a dog and if he has toys around the house and is in on his own and a little bit bored why can't he have your toys, the ones you keep on the radiator? He doesn't stop to think that they're actually a pair of socks and that he isn't allowed to touch them; he has the run of the house or the freedom of the room with nobody but him in it, so for a short time he can make his own decisions. He's been told not to touch or carry shoes around but that was the other day and did he really understand that this meant he was never to touch them? With socks to throw around and shoes to chew life suddenly becomes more exciting, and rather than chew anything else soft the chair leg seems a far better challenge – and of course once he's excited the bladder and the bowels go into overdrive and suddenly the door opens and in you walk, and he's so happy to see you and show you what he has achieved. Unless, of course, this isn't the first time – in which case his memory will suddenly kick in and tell him you are going to be cross but he isn't really sure why as you have given him all the things to do again that you don't want him to do.

SUMMARY

Pause and think, and no matter how upset you may be, you will be much better able to communicate with your dog if you keep your body calm and relaxed. Don't be tempted to try to tell him what he's done wrong and why he shouldn't have done it as he won't understand; he will understand only that you are not happy, but he won't be sure why. Try to see things from your dog's perspective and give him time to fully understand what you are trying to achieve with him.

METHODS

Watch his body language, for dogs deserve the same observation they give to us. If his body is moving with rapid and short movements, and he has lost his suppleness, he will have become overexcited. Keep him quiet and give him a positive body language to observe and he will soon calm down, and with time out for both of you it will be easier to work out how and why he became stressed. It is always better to try to prevent misbehaviour than to try to cure it, as once a dog has done something it will remain in his memory and each time it surfaces it will remind him of your previous response to the action. If he remembers that you were annoyed with him he will react as he did at the time and you will wonder why he is looking worried, but if he remembers how much fun it was he will be tempted to do it again, even if it wasn't fun for you. The dog's memory bank, which is explained in a later chapter, has to be managed very carefully to encourage the positive memories and discourage those that can cause undesirable behaviour.

CASE HISTORY – JENNY

Jenny was a quiet little dog and very sensitive. She was running off lead in a park when her guardian called her back. Jenny had been running towards another dog and when she turned to come back she saw a stiff body, with arms waving wildly at her. She panicked, thinking she was being told off, and ran in a circle to come behind her guardian, who threw her arms in the air to make Jenny run faster towards her. Her guardian interpreted Jenny's action as disobedience and was annoyed with her, but Jenny thought her guardian was angry and came in behind her as a mark of respect. When she saw arms waving rapidly in the air it was as if she was being shouted at and she became confused – and in her panic she nipped her owner. Jenny was no longer wanted and came into rescue. It took several weeks of very gentle body language for Jenny to learn to trust again and for a long time she would cower if she saw someone waving their arms, as her memory would make her want to nip but being a sensitive nonaggressive dog she knew this was wrong and would then become very submissive. The incident in the park had taken just a few moments of time and had been caused by incorrect body language, but it took many months for Jenny to be completely over what had happened to her.

5 KEEPING THE BASICS SIMPLE

There are four golden rules a mother will teach her pups: to remain in the den and not come out until she says it's safe to do so; to follow behind her until she says it's safe to go ahead; to keep their attention on her; and to come back when she calls them. With these rules the puppies can mature into an adolescent pack with a foundation of good manners and ready to learn more. A puppy that leaves the pen and goes ahead without permission, ignores his mother's yap for attention and refuses to come back when she calls him is not only putting himself in danger but is putting the other pups, his mother and the rest of the pack at risk. What would happen in the pack is not dissimilar to what could happen

in the home; a puppy that pushes ahead without permission is taking control, and if he refuses to pay attention and doesn't come back when called he is certainly at risk, not from predators but from traffic, other dogs and getting lost if he roams too far. With those four golden rules lead walking becomes easy, a dog will never roam far from his guardian and he will come running back the moment he hears his name called. The rules are not difficult to teach if they are kept simple and if a dog is given time to understand what is expected of him. But they are not negotiable; they are the guidelines for a dog to live by and for him to be a wonderful loyal and attentive companion while preserving his free spirit. Most

Lead walking is more important than high fives or retrieving a ball. Note the relaxed hands on the lead transmitting a calm signal to the dog, who becomes just as relaxed.

A very wise old Border Collie with a wonderful temperament, and throughout his working life Loch flatly refused to sit down, waiting until he was a retired old gent.

of what he will learn later can be negotiable – for example, does he really have to sit and stay, or can he stand if he prefers, and does he have to give a high five if he doesn't want to or will you settle for a handshake or wave? The more solid the foundation of the four non-negotiable commands, the more willing he is likely to be to do the things you ask in further training as you will have learned to think like him and speak his language, making training much easier and more companionable for you both.

A lot of dogs with behavioural issues, such as aggression, running off, awkwardness with other dogs or people, jumping up at strangers, being difficult with visitors to the house, etc., are able to give a paw, do a high five, roll over and play dead, and fetch a ball, and they know all the toys in the toy box. The things they can't do are: walk sensibly on a lead; come back when called; and go through doorways calmly without pushing someone over. They rarely, if ever, look at or pay attention to their guardians when out on a walk, preferring to sniff the grass verge or play with other dogs. They have been trained to do things that are fun but unimportant to begin with, and have not been taught the four golden rules; had these been applied, such dogs could still do all the high fives and fetch games at a later date but they would not have the behavioural problems.

THE IMPORTANCE OF FIRM FOUNDATIONS

No dog is perfect. They all have some issues or problems, but training a dog is like building a house: with a poor foundation every crack becomes a major flaw, but with a good foundation even a major crack can soon be repaired.

The secret lies not in trying to teach your dog by making him do something, but instead in telling him what is he doing and then teaching him a command for that action. A dog will always want to go ahead through a door if he thinks there is something to rush through for, but teaching him to have a little restraint by asking him to sit and

wait means he has to learn two commands before he can go through a door. A dog will struggle to learn two things at once, unless it's something he fully understands and really wants to do, so it's far better to teach the whole process of not pushing through doors with one command, issued in a way he will recognize immediately, using body language.

WAITING AT A DOOR

The best way to make sure that a dog doesn't push out of the door before you is to go through

If a dog is asked to sit before going through a door or gate, he is responding to your command and not the urge to rush ahead. Tess is responding to the sit but is looking ahead and will walk out expecting to lead the way.

key word you want him to associate with being well-mannered at the door. Now you can negotiate. If you think he will walk out calmly with you, go through the door – but the chances are he will rush out so to remain in control move to one side and tell him he can go out. Now if he rushes through the door, it is with your permission. A Border Collie has a wonderful free spirit and the last thing you want to do is to crush or dominate that spirit; he will work with you and for you if he understands what you want of him, and is able to work out for himself what is the best line of action to take. With this simple technique in a

When Tess receives a message she understands – the simple movement of the handler's body in front of her – she immediately responds to her handler.

When the handler's body moves to one side Tess is still engaged in 'conversation' and is waiting so they can go out together. Note how relaxed they both are.

it first, or negotiate as to how and when he goes through. Put him on a lead and before you open the door stand him behind you and don't let his nose get in front of, or to the side of, your legs. The secret is believing in yourself and what you are doing: you are taking away his option of rushing out in front of you and you are not wasting words he doesn't understand. As soon as he stands calmly, tell him what a good dog he is. Even though you are blocking him, it becomes his wish to stop trying to pass you; he has chosen to stand still behind you, so you can give him any doorway, he quickly understands that he lets you go through first, which puts you in a leadership position and encourages trust and confidence in your relationship with him. His reward is that, after you have checked to make sure that everything at the other side of the door is safe for him, he can go out and enjoy the freedom you have just given him permission to have. Try this to begin with going from one room to another, and then from the house to the garden, and remember that your body remains strong in the fact that you won't give in and let him push you aside, but gentle and flowing with every movement to give him confidence in you. When a dog stands back at the door to let you check ahead for him, you know he is giving you respect as a leader or parent figure, and that will make him feel a secure and loved dog. If you are not consistent, doing it

Taken back to have a discussion about good manners, Rosie immediately begins to engage with the handler. Note how the handler's body portrays a stronger message to Rosie than was needed with Tess.

Rosie is on a mission: she is first out of the gate and is turning to the right, taking control. The handler's body is not as relaxed, as the pace is being dictated by Rosie.

only on days when you have time and letting him rush out on other days, you are giving him mixed messages and training him will take much longer. A dog needs to store in his memory what you want of him, so that each time he sees or hears a trigger it reminds him of that memory and he will know how to react.

THE MEMORY BANK

Understanding a dog's memory can give a valuable insight into why a dog may suddenly act unpredictably, perhaps taking a sudden dislike to someone or something without any prior warning. Our memories are stored and we can bring them back whenever we want; we can make ourselves laugh, cry, feel happy or sad just by bringing up a memory from an event or action from our past. A dog's memory bank is a little different; they don't remember all their past, and they cannot bring events or actions back into their mind at will. But a trigger will bring a memory that can cause an unexpected reaction in a dog and it can be anything: a smell, a tone of voice, a certain action such as a hand movement, or something visual, for example another dog or a person. It's important to be able to work out what the trigger is and the best way is by observation, and even by making notes of when, where and to what your dog is reacting. It helps to think of the memory as a deck of cards, and the unwanted behaviour as one particular card; for example, if the unwanted behaviour is the ace of spades, each time that card is played it rises to the top of the pack. The way to 'lose' the ace of spades is to keep playing other cards until it is almost at the bottom of the pack; it is still there but it is not in any danger of being played. What is in a dog's memory cannot be erased but it can be managed if, as in the deck of cards analogy, triggers for unwanted behaviour can be moved down the pack by not allowing them to be played in his present-day mind.

It isn't always easy to keep a dog away from the triggers if they are part of an everyday occurrence; it can be difficult, for example, to avoid other dogs, traffic and people, but when a dog has a fear of something that makes him react, in either a nervous or an aggressive way, the first thing to work on is trust, and it's difficult for a dog to learn to trust if he is constantly being confronted by what worries him.

TEACHING A DOG TO SIT

Teaching simple commands such as 'sit' and 'wait' can be part of everyday life and don't require special training sessions. The secret is to wait until

---

CASE HISTORY – LADDIE'S MEMORY TRIGGERS

Laddie had a bad start in life and had been abused. It didn't take long to discover that he reacted aggressively to men wearing caps and men with beards, but it was several weeks before a third memory trigger emerged. Laddie was happy in the company of my two young children but one day when I took him with me to collect them from junior school, he began to growl at them the moment they got in the car. This was an unexpected reaction, and as soon as we were home and they were playing outside he was fine. After a second growling session, I took some clothes for them to change into before they got into the car, removing the carbolic-smelling school ones to the car boot, and Laddie was fine, with not a single growl. Care was taken not to play the 'bad cards', which, in the case of the smell, meant that when my son and daughter came home from junior school they had to change before they saw Laddie, men had to remove their caps and Laddie had to be removed from the room before a man with a beard could enter! It took a long time, but I kept those memories dormant by not allowing the 'bad card' to be played and instead kept playing good cards. Laddie loved working sheep so he learned a new skill; he loved playing football with my son (apparently he was a first-class goalkeeper!) and he would sit for hours watching the hens and ducks. During that time we worked on building up a relationship of trust and finally, after several months of me refusing to let the bad memories surface, Laddie was very slowly reintroduced to memories of his past. He wasn't asked to do anything other than walk past and ignore men with caps or beards, but after several more months Laddie became confident enough to let them work him on sheepdog handling courses.

Teaching a word to an action is much easier than trying to make a dog commit an action to a word. On seeing a dog about to sit, say the word you want him to associate with the action. As this dog sits on his own accord, he hears the word 'sit'.

Gently stroking a dog until he wants to sit down will give the action you need for the sit command: here, gentle stroking has the dog wanting to sit. Good manners training doesn't need special training sessions and should be part of everyday life.

he is doing something you want and then give him the appropriate 'sound' or command. Pushing a dog down to make him sit usually results in the dog resisting and pushing up. Saying the word 'sit' each time the dog sits on his own accord, and then calmly praising him, encourages word association.

By trying to *make* your dog sit to teach him the word command, you are putting two things into his memory: doing the action and remembering the key word. But when he sits because he wants to and each time hears the key word as he does so, he is only learning one thing – the word you want him to associate with the action he is doing. Eventually he will hear the word 'sit' and do the action the word reminds him of. Trying to speed up the process by making him sit by pushing him into position can cause confusion that may slow his training progress, because the hands that usually stroke him are suddenly pushing him down. Putting your hand under his chin and gently easing him back while you stroke him will make him want to sit, and as he does he hears the key word 'sit'. Puppies spend a lot of time sitting on their own accord; this makes training easier and they are very responsive to the hand under the chin encouragement, but if an older dog doesn't respond to sitting, meet him halfway by encouraging word association to 'stand', and as your relationship progresses he will learn to sit for you.

It's very easy to use body language that makes sense to us, but to a dog it's only adding further confusion, for example pointing to the floor to get a dog to lie down, waving our arms about for him to come back when called, and clapping when he does well. We have our own language which we try to make our dogs understand, but we also ask them to learn a body language that isn't familiar to them at all. We are expecting them to learn two forms of communication, neither of which they know, when we really need to get to know what they are thinking so we can turn their thought process to our advantage when asking them to do something for us, which we are doing every time we teach them something new. To do this we are the ones that need to learn their language so we can communicate with them in a way they understand, thus making teaching good manners and further training not only much easier but good fun.

TEACHING A DOG TO LIE DOWN

Many Border Collies prefer lying down to sitting and to begin with you should go with whatever he prefers; for basic good manners training it really doesn't matter which he does, but make sure you don't waste words that you may want to use at a later date. For example, if he really doesn't seem to want to sit and you keep trying to make him, he will begin to resent both the action and the word. Once you have him a little further on with his training he may surprise you one day by sitting when you least expect it. But if in his memory he still has a resentment of the word 'sit', the minute you use it he will move, and it may be a long time before he does sit willingly for you. This word association can apply to any word or action he has stored in his memory bank, so care needs to be taken for him not to store unwanted memories.

Choose a command that you will only use for the action you want. If 'lie down' or 'down' is the one you want to use, it must be kept for that action and not used to stop the dog from jumping up or onto furniture. Your dog will lie down quite often on his own accord and that is when you need to tell him what he is doing. Dogs aren't automatically tuned into human tones so it's better to give a double-barrelled command, such as 'lie down', to help get his attention. Put a house lead on him when you sit down and bring him to your side, give him a stroke and then let him settle; with his options to roam gone, he will soon lie down and as he goes down give him the command. It's no good giving a command before or after an action – it needs to be at the precise moment the dog does it, which is why observing and understanding your dog's movement is important. Try to resist the urge to point to the floor each time as you may find later that the command is ignored if you don't point.

What you are thinking
You may think that teaching the lie down com-

mand by pointing to the floor gives a clear indication of what is wanted of your dog, and by lowering the tone of your voice he will eventually understand; and if not, a gentle push down will encourage him to lie down. To make him sit you may think that by constantly repeating the word 'sit' and pushing his rump downwards, he will understand exactly what you want.

What your dog is thinking

Pointing to the floor often indicates a titbit, a food dish or a ball; although the tone of voice has changed, your dog doesn't recognize what you are saying – you just sound different and he has no reason to associate it with lying down. When you push him down to try to get him to sit, he is pushing up, so any word association is with

Use every opportunity to communicate with your dog and to teach him something new. Out on a walk, if a young dog turns round and stands still to see what is happening next, it is an ideal opportunity to issue the 'wait' instruction.

resistance, not compliance. Constantly repeating the word and then praising him when, after several attempts, he finally does it means he gets rewarded after hearing the same word several times.

TEACHING A DOG TO WAIT

You have a choice of 'wait' or 'stay', but to begin with you need to keep things simple. To achieve a 'stay', your dog first needs to understand how to sit or lie down, so try not to begin teaching something that has to interact with another command. The simpler and more uncomplicated you can make your training, the easier it will be for your dog to learn. Teaching your dog simple commands needs to be a part of everyday life; as you stand in front of him in the doorway, he hears the word 'wait'. When you are walking him on a lead, keep stopping and when he stops he hears the word 'stand'. When he understands this, make a slight movement as if you are going to take a step forward but don't actually take the step; your dog will notice your movement and start to move to go with you. Before he does so, hold the lead so that he remains still and tell him to 'wait', pause for a moment and then invite him to move forwards with you.

Teaching your dog a command with words and actions he doesn't understand is hard work and can be confusing for your dog; instead watch what he does and tell him what he is doing, concentrating on one command at a time. Once your dog has a solid foundation of basic good manners, during which time you will have learned to understand him and what he is thinking, then you can begin more complicated training without confusing him or making it difficult for yourself.

MEAL-TIME

Meal-times for a dog need to be kept as simple as his training. There are many different approaches, from taking your dog's dish of food away, to pretending to eat some of it first, and it is often considered better not to feed your dog until

TRAINING THE NATURAL WAY

When training a dog to work sheep, a shepherd doesn't begin by telling the dog the commands for left and right, but simply lets the dog move around the sheep. When the dog begins to use his natural instinct to keep a small flock together, the shepherd begins to move in a circle, to left and right, keeping the sheep in the centre. In his desire to keep the sheep held to the shepherd, the dog will move in the same direction in an attempt to keep opposite him, and whichever direction the dog goes in he will hear the corresponding command. In this simple exercise the shepherd is teaching the dog to learn how to respond to him in order to do his job, how to work out a situation and also the commands that he needs to understand. In time he will hear the

A shepherd teaches his dog commands by using body language first, and he starts off in a controlled area with a small number of sheep. He will not rush his dog or try to teach too many things at once.

command and respond by going in the direction he is used to going in when he has heard it previously. Encouraging a dog to do something of his own accord and then telling him what he is doing is a very simple and uncomplicated way of training.

after you have eaten. However, you are trying to build a relationship with your dog so to keep taking his food away, even if only for a few seconds, after you have given it to him isn't a very good way to build trust. Would you keep taking away a child's dinner? With a good relationship and trust your dog will let you take the dish if you need to, but without that need he deserves to be able to eat it in peace. If you are going to feed him after you have eaten, which meal will you use as a guideline – breakfast, lunch or your evening meal? If you are in control of the home and you are his pack leader or parent figure, it shouldn't make any difference whether you feed him before or after you eat, or at the start, middle or end of the day. If you have more than one dog it

is better to feed them in separate areas or rooms, or in their own space or Dog Dens. Even with dogs that get on really well together, a problem may develop if they eat at different speeds; each dog deserves to be able to enjoy his meal in peace and at a pace that suits him, without always having to keep a wary eye on another dog.

If you make an issue out of meal-times there is a danger it will escalate and become a real problem, so keep it simple but well-mannered. You will be feeding your dog from day one when he won't know either 'sit' or 'stay', so begin by telling him what he is doing. A puppy will often sit or stand when he sees the dish coming, and a calm older dog may wait patiently while you pre-

59

pare his meal and present him with his dish, but sometimes an older dog may not be as obliging, choosing to try to take his food without showing any good manners. When he has the incentive of a dish of food in front of him he may not be inclined to want to listen to you telling him he has stop and wait before tucking in. Take him out of the room, put his dish on the floor and then bring him in with a lead threaded through his collar. Stand him still for a matter of seconds at a distance from the dish (too near and the temptation to pull to the dish may be too great), tell him to 'wait' and then give him permission to go and enjoy his meal, allowing the lead to slip out of the collar as he goes forwards.

TONE OF VOICE

Try to keep your voice as normal as possible when you talk to your dog. If you vary your voice from a very low tone to a high-pitched one, he will have to process those variations as well as your normal tone. It's better to make your commands clear and indicative of what you want with your natural voice, rather than putting on a different one, and try to resist the urge to issue your commands at a higher volume than normal. Your dog can hear you whisper and so your normal voice will be quite loud to him, which means that if all your commands are issued at a higher volume he will think you are shouting. The range of frequencies that dogs can hear is much greater than humans can hear, and because of this dogs can have a difficult time with very loud noises. Sounds that may be tolerable to you can be uncomfortable for a dog's more sensitive hearing; for example, a noise that you can hear from 20 metres away, your dog could detect at 80 metres, and the sound of the vacuum cleaner, washing machine or car engine, which you find acceptable, may have a loud annoying pitch to your dog.

Even though we know that dogs don't understand our language, we still talk to them. This is a good thing as our mood changes with our conversation, and the energy we produce with each mood will tell our dogs what we are feeling. So if you speak in a soft voice to your dog when in normal conversation and when you are telling him what he means to you, he will respond to your tone and your emotions. When you want him to be calm, speak slowly and keep your tone even, without being too high or too low. If you keep your 'happy tones' at an interesting but calm level – for example, instead of a simple 'good dog' tell him how well he is doing and how proud of him you are – he will respond with your mirror image. He will be a calm, happy and proud dog.

SOCIALIZATION

Dogs need to feel comfortable in the world around them, so they do need to see and get used to different sights, sounds and smells, but

TRAINING WITH A WHISPER

After a winning run at a sheepdog trial, a shepherd was asked by a spectator how he trained his dog, and what was his secret to having a dog that did everything he asked at the first time of asking, when he never raised his voice above a normal pitch. The shepherd replied, 'There is no secret. I train him with a whisper which he can easily hear but the further away he goes the more he has to concentrate on listening to me. The result is a dog who has his attention on me and listens to all I say, but if I raised my voice to how you command your dog, my dog would take it as a reprimand.' The fascinated spectator asked if it did not pose a problem in everyday life when he spoke in his normal voice. The bemused shepherd replied, 'Nay, lad, I always speak quietly to him when I use my voice but you don't need a voice to speak to a dog; he will listen to my body but most of the time we're in each other's minds.'

Spending quality time with your dog and speaking to him in a soft voice not only strengthens the bond between you but will encourage him to respond to both your voice and your emotions.

remember that the confidence to be at ease with everything they meet comes from trust rather than from a possible overload of introductions. A puppy doesn't investigate anything new until his mother has checked it for safety, in just the same way that parents wouldn't let their young child approach, or be approached by, strangers. Meeting people and being introduced to new things are important to an extent, but allowing a dog to approach any dog or person he meets may not only lead to him making his own decisions about how to react, but also encourage bad manners. A

dog's natural instinct is to sit back and weigh up a situation; he uses his senses of sight and hearing, and more importantly his sense of smell. Of all a dog's senses, his sense of smell is the most highly developed, dogs having about twenty times more olfactory receptors than humans do. When a dog is approaching, or being approached by, another dog or a person he doesn't know, his sense of smell sets to work to provide the information needed to enable him to know how to deal with the situation – whether to meet and greet or to keep a safe distance. This takes time, which is why dogs will stand at a distance from something they are not sure of, allowing their senses to process all the information available. If a dog is encouraged to run straight up to everyone he meets, and to approach other dogs without first standing back and using his sense of smell, he is being prevented from using his natural instincts, which would provide the information he needs as to who he may or may not get on with, and whether an approaching dog is going to be friendly or hostile. A dog that is not encouraged to stop and think and seek

Lad's senses are keener than his handler's and he has picked up something in front that he would like to investigate.

The object of Lad's attention is a cat. Note how the handler has moved Lad behind him and is standing with one leg across the front of him. With this one simple movement, although Lad is still looking at the cat, he is beginning to relax and disengage from it. This is good training for when he is out and about meeting people and seeing other dogs.

permission to approach other people and dogs can soon become bad-mannered, jumping up at strangers and approaching other dogs regardless of their age or status. At best this can be upsetting, but sadly it can also get the dog into trouble and even into a fight with other dogs.

Lack of socialization is often given as the reason why some dogs are insecure or have behavioural issues, but over-socialization can cause more problems. A dog doesn't have to be socialized to be at ease with people he doesn't know; as long as he trusts his guardian, he will go almost anywhere and meet anyone.

FAMILIARIZATION

Rather than rushing to socialize your dog, it is better to familiarize him with the world around him and give him the idea that although he will see people and other dogs, they are not a major part of his life. A dog who focuses on something or somebody other than his guardian will often cease to listen and refuse to be recalled. A dog who is used to seeing other people and dogs but not always approaching or interacting with them will soon learn to wait until invited to interact. If you show your dog everything he is likely to meet and make an issue of it, he will soon come to believe that everything is a problem. For example, showing your dog the neighbour's dog or cat and saying 'no' is as good as telling your dog that there is a dog or cat there, and it could be an issue. But a well-mannered dog who understands that he doesn't go chasing off and making his own decisions may be fully aware of the dog or cat but he won't react to them as long as they don't invade his space.

JUMPING UP AND BARKING

What may be acceptable behaviour in a puppy can pose a problem when a dog is fully grown. Teach your dog not to jump up at people by standing him behind you for a few moments before giving him permission to meet and greet. He will soon learn he has to be invited to greet someone, and that he only gets stroked when he is standing calmly and not when he jumps up.

There is nothing wrong with a dog barking in response to a knock on the door, but he should then stand back and let you attend to the visitors. If he tries to jump up at the door or at the visitors as they enter, remove him from the area before you open the door but never hold him by, or pull on, his collar. Put a lead on him and take him calmly to another room, preferably his own area; then, when the visitors are settled, he can be invited back into their company. He doesn't greet them immediately; instead he sits on his 'Chill Mat' (see Chapter 6) and waits to be invited to meet and greet.

SUMMARY

Don't try to make a dog do something he doesn't understand. Instead gently encourage him to do something and then tell him what he is doing. Don't try to give him too much information at once; for example, he doesn't have to sit and wait at a door unless he understands both commands. Standing and waiting is perfectly acceptable and less confusing for a dog who is struggling to understand.

Socialization is not as important as creating a relationship with your dog and familiarizing him with everything around him, rather than introducing him to everything too soon.

Understanding how a dog may see a situation differently from you is important and will help to manage his memory bank.

METHODS

Keep your voice calm and speak quietly, and don't keep repeating a command, thinking that your dog will learn from repetition. All he will learn is that he only needs do something when you have asked him several times.

Only ask your dog to do something you know you can both achieve. For example, you can teach him to 'wait' by standing still with him; once he is used to this, he may even sit when he understands that he is not moving forwards immediately. You can then tell him what he is doing by giving the 'sit' command at the moment he does it.

Don't try to control your dog by controlling his feeding regime. He is entitled to be able to eat his meals in peace, but equally don't let him control you by dictating how long he will take to eat it. If he doesn't seem to be hungry, providing he is a fit dog with no health issues, don't change his diet straight away but instead try giving a little less food next time as he probably doesn't need the amount you are giving. If he is gulping his food because he is worried it may be taken from him (this usually happens when dogs are fed with other dogs, or when people are standing watching), try feeding him in his own area; make sure no other dog or cat is around and leave him to eat in peace.

CASE HISTORY – BARNEY'S COLLAR ISSUE

Barney was used to having his own way. He pulled on a lead and jumped up at everyone he met, including strangers; he also ran up to other dogs on a walk and was constantly getting into trouble. The problems escalated one day when Barney began jumping up and barking at a visitor. His guardian took hold of the back of his collar and tried to pull him back from the door. The more he pulled, the more Barney barked – and as tempers flared Barney turned on his guardian and bit his hand.

When two dogs are focused on the same possession – which can be anything from a bone or a toy to a moving prey such as a rabbit – they will fight for it, and the one not in possession will sink his teeth into the back of the neck of the other to make him let go. If someone takes hold of the back of a dog's collar when he is wound up and over-excited, his mind interprets the scenario as him being the one in possession and the person holding the collar as the competitor trying to take it from him.

Barney's training programme included learning not to pull on a lead and to stand calmly to be stroked. When someone knocked on the door, he was told he was a good boy for barking and then he had a lead put on him and he was taken into another room. To begin with his guardian had to use a slip lead as it was the only way he could remove him quickly and quietly, and for the first few lessons a friend knocked on the door but didn't enter. This way Barney learned very calmly and without any stress how to behave, and he also discovered that, although he was praised for letting people know that someone was knocking on the door, he had to wait to be invited to meet the visitor.

Never try to control a dog by pulling on the back of his collar. In the heat of the moment a dog may react adversely, or pull or lunge forwards even more. Barney had been in this position so many times that as soon as someone took hold of his collar, he would look for something to react to.

6 THE 'CHILL MAT'

The 'Chill Mat' is probably one of the most important things you can have for your dog and is the simplest one to introduce. It works for dogs of any age, with or without behavioural problems, and is the key to a calm dog.

If you want a dog to stop doing something, you have to provide him with an alternative, more acceptable option. For example, a dog who won't leave visitors alone can be removed from the room, which solves the immediate problem but doesn't teach him how to behave, so the problem will recur. If you teach your dog to sit calmly on his 'Chill Mat', you have provided an alternative for him, which means he can stay in the room, sit quietly on his mat and learn how to behave when you have visitors. We can draw a parallel with children displaying unacceptable behaviour; they are corrected and given an example of acceptable behaviour. For example, a child shouting and being disruptive will respond better to being told to stop shouting and sit down and read a book or play quietly than if they were only told to be quiet.

The 'Chill Mat' is a piece of vet bed belonging to your dog. If you have more than one dog, buy vet beds of different colours to prevent you from making the mistake of asking your dogs to sit on the wrong mats. It has to be separate from your dog's bed and must be a different mat or vet bed from what he usually lies on, and it is only used to calm your dog – not to make him feel isolated.

Your dog's bed should be in his area and it should remain static so he knows that whatever happens in his life his bed will always be in the same place. In addition to his main bed he may have other beds, and certainly one in the room you spend most time in. The 'Chill Mat', however, is completely different: it doesn't have a set area to be in, and it is only put on the floor when it is needed.

WHY A 'CHILL MAT'?

There will be few, if any, dogs who have not at some time been told to go to their bed because they have pushed a boundary. You may have had to put your puppy in his bed or his Dog Den to get him to sleep or to calm him down when he became over-excited. As an adult dog he may have barked at someone coming into your house and been sent to his bed until your visitor had come in and sat down, or he might have been testing his teeth on a shoe or a piece of furniture. It is no different from sending a child to their bedroom to calm down and think about their behaviour; it doesn't make the bed or the bedroom an unpleasant place – on the contrary it makes it a safe haven where the miscreant can either sleep peacefully or wait until everything is calm enough for them to go back into the family unit. For a dog his bed is the place where he goes voluntarily to sleep, or he is sent there because he's pushed a boundary. To exclude a dog because he has exhibited unacceptable behaviour isn't teaching him either how to behave or what is acceptable behaviour. Each time he is about to try to chase a rabbit on the television screen he isn't going to think that maybe he should leave the room instead. Border Collies are very clever and very quick to learn, but they need to have things explained to them very simply and providing a 'Chill Mat' is the equivalent of a child's bean bag or cushion: it's the in-between stage that says be quiet and calm down and you won't need to go to your bed. Prevention is better than cure and by watching your dog closely during his formative training you will be able to interrupt any move on his part towards an action that you don't want him to display, and gently show him an alternative.

HOW THE 'CHILL MAT' WORKS

Dogs love territories, areas they can mark as theirs; it makes them feel safe but it also gives them a feeling of belonging. In your mind you know he belongs and that he can have the freedom of your home, but if you don't make it clear to him that it is your home, there is a possibility that in his mind he will think you are sharing it, giving him equal rights, and if he is a strong dog he might want to take over. You may have strict rules that mean your dog doesn't go upstairs or sit on the furniture, but if he believes he owns or has equal share of the kitchen and hallway, he will respect the banned areas but believe he is free to be destructive in the areas he perceives to be his. On the other hand, there may be no strict rules and he has access to all the rooms, his bed might be in your bedroom and he might get on your bed during the night, but if he is fully aware that the home, the rooms and the bed are yours and that he has access to them all with your permission, he may be better behaved and less destructive than if he only has rules for half of the house. You don't need a lot of house rules – you just need to make him understand that it is your house and not a huge play area for him to do as he pleases in. By providing him with his own 'Chill Mat', which will become his mark, you are giving him something he can understand and will learn quickly.

When you go into your room in the evening put a light lead on your dog, place the Mat down by your feet and ask him to lie on it. The purpose of the lead is to make sure that he doesn't keep getting up and wandering around, forcing you to have to keep repeating your request. He can be stroked and gently massaged while he is on his Mat, but to begin with just let him sit quietly; if he thinks the aim is for him to get attention, you will be defeating the object of the exercise. When he is settled put the lead down so that he can wander off if he wants, or he may prefer to stay where he is; either is fine, as long as he has sat calmly for a short while first and you have given him permission to wander off (when you disengage from the lead). It is not a training exercise, so never leave him on the Mat while you leave the room, and never make him sit on it for longer than he needs to. The 'Chill Mat's main function is, literally, to chill him out and give him his own portable safe area.

Once your dog becomes used to settling on his 'Chill Mat', he will know that when you put the mat on the floor it's time for him to settle down.

THE ROLE OF THE 'CHILL MAT'

If you have a nervous dog, he may be very timid about entering a room that is unfamiliar to him, or where there are people he doesn't know; he will be out of his comfort zone and will feel very vulnerable. If he has a bed in the room he may go and sit in it but in essence he is hiding and not learning how to relax. But his 'Chill Mat', when he has become used to it, means he can sit with his guardian and calm down, as being safe will be the first thing that enters his mind once he sits on it. He can be stroked while he relaxes, in the knowledge that while he is on that Mat nobody but his family will touch him and the visitors will leave him alone. He is in his own safe zone and can remain in the room knowing there is nothing to worry about.

If you have a strong or wilful dog he will probably want to rush into any room where there is an open door and jump up at visitors. But when he becomes used to the 'Chill Mat' he will understand that he can't go into a room and do as he pleases; he has to seek permission to have the freedom of the room by sitting quietly for a few moments on his Mat. When visitors are present, he has to sit on his Mat and wait to be invited to go to them, and if asked to come back to the Mat he must do so straight away.

You must be very calm and patient while you are teaching your dog the purpose of his 'Chill Mat', as rushing the process can ruin how he perceives the Mat. Once he understands that it is his invisible cocoon of safety, it will become the most valuable piece of equipment you have for him. It will go with you when you are visiting friends, when you take him on holiday, when he goes to work with you, or on a family picnic to remind him that he can't jump into the picnic basket and devour its contents. What you don't do is take it somewhere where you know your dog is likely to be upset: for example, never ask him to sit on his 'Chill Mat' at the vets when he is going to have a vaccination. His Mat is intended to make him feel safe, and if the insertion of a needle or some medication is inevitable, his trust in his Mat will come into question.

Unlike the bed, the 'Chill Mat' can be moved anywhere, so if you have visitors and your dog doesn't like too much attention he has no need to leave the room because he can settle wherever you put his mat and he will feel safe.

The 'Chill Mat' is everyone's best friend. A nervous dog doesn't have to leave the garden when the family are having a get-together; instead he can sit quietly on the patio on his Mat. Likewise, a boisterous dog knows he has to calm down.

THE END OF THE 'CHILL MAT'S USE

The use of the 'Chill Mat' never comes to an end, but there will come a time when it is only needed occasionally. We can liken it to teaching a child the rule of not taking the last biscuit from a plate, but if extra conditions are added to that rule, such as 'unless there are more in the tin', 'nobody else likes it', or 'it will go soft if it isn't eaten', the basic rule becomes lost in all the variables. It is a simple rule not to take the last biscuit but there is never a designated time when a child needs teaching when they can take the last biscuit because as they grow up they move into the grey area of knowing when rules can be broken without displaying bad manners. Dogs need clear rules and boundaries to enable them to live in the grey area, but if they live in that grey area because they don't know any better, they can soon develop behavioural problems. Once your dog fully understands the 'Chill Mat', he will often calm down or settle to the words 'Chill time', and the actual Mat will only need to be used when you are away from home or a new visitor arrives. In the case history below, once Paddy was fully trained his 'Chill Mat' spent more time on the arm of the sofa than on the floor, but for a long time it was always nearby as a gentle reminder that at certain times he was expected to settle down and be a good lad.

CASE HISTORY – PADDY AND THE TELEVISION

Paddy was young and full of energy, and had become used to treating his home like a huge playground. His behaviour of chasing anything that moved hadn't really worried his guardians too much and his favourite pastime of stalking the television screen had caused amusement both to them and to visitors. But things came to a head one evening when Paddy charged at the television set when he saw horses galloping across the screen. He caused a lot of damage but his guardians were more concerned that the behaviour they had thought to be harmless had suddenly proved dangerous.

Every evening Paddy was taken in the living room and a 'Chill Mat' was placed on the floor by his guardian's feet. To begin with Paddy refused to stay still but, with his lead on, his options were limited to only being able to move around on the mat and he soon settled. It took only two evenings of sitting calmly on his 'Chill Mat' for Paddy to actually look forward to going into the room and sitting quietly and being stroked and talked to. The next stage was to reintroduce the television, and it was switched on to a programme that was selected as being the least likely to excite him. Each time Paddy thought it might be good to investigate the television he was told 'no' and asked to stay on his mat and be stroked. It took a week of careful training but Paddy quickly learned that if he felt the urge to run to the television, he had to look at his guardian and seek guidance from her as to what he should do instead. Learning how to be calm in the home and to take guidance from his guardian also provided Paddy with a good foundation for learning how to listen when out on a walk, paving the way for teaching him lead walking and recall.

7 LEAD TRAINING

Lead training is one of the most important aspects of training, but it often gets overlooked or dismissed as something to aim for at a later date. But the later it is left, the more difficult it can become, not because it is difficult to teach but because a dog will have become set in his ways, and having spent his time always leading the way he may resent suddenly being told he is not in control. Remember the four golden rules in the previous chapter. The word 'lead' has several meanings: to guide, to go in front, to show the way and to go ahead. Dogs who become used to the role of leading either take control or feel they are being left in control, and should a problem arise while out on a walk they will make the decision about how to deal with it. The dog that takes control will begin to pull more and more on a lead and may become dominant and even show aggression to other dogs or even to people. The dog who feels he is being left in control will often feel insecure, and if any aggression is shown it will be born of nerves. Even if an incident doesn't occur to make either over-confidence or insecurity arise, a dog who pulls is rarely a pleasure to walk on a lead, which often means they are left to run loose whenever possible. But dogs who pull on a lead rarely have a reliable recall, and a dog who doesn't come back when called can find himself in trouble: he may meet another loose dog that proves to be aggressive; he may run across a busy road; or he may simply become lost a long way from home. Whether the problem is an aggressive dog or a nervous one, or a dog who doesn't come back when called, the problem either wouldn't exist or would be more easily manageable if he had learned how to walk correctly on a lead.

HOW A DOG TAKES CONTROL

Teaching a dog to walk on a lead has several purposes and it's not just a case of making it easier when going for a walk. It's about teaching

A dog pulling on a lead is a dog taking control. Both dog and handler are in forward motion and the handler has no balance to bring the dog back under control; with the lead at full length, there is a risk that the dog will break loose.

respect and good manners, rather like teaching a child how to behave in company. A dog pulling on a lead and dragging someone along the grass verge while he sniffs the ground is like trying to have a conversation with someone busy texting on a mobile phone. Ironically, what would be considered bad manners in a human, whether child or adult, is often accepted in a dog. A child having a tantrum, screaming and dragging at his parent's arm in the local supermarket, draws not only attention but often criticism. However, the same kind of tantrum from a dog dragging his guardian along the grass verge while he accosts every other dog and person he comes across is often ignored because he's 'just a dog' and he doesn't understand. But he will believe that he is in control because he hasn't been taught to understand anything different. He is leading the way so in his mind he is entitled to do as he pleases, and the chances are he will be in control in other areas of his life as well as when out on a walk. It's easy for someone to slip into an accept-

ance of lead pulling as it can become a habit for both dog and guardian, but it's a habit that, even if it doesn't have repercussions, greatly reduces the chances of a pleasant and peaceful walk. Preventing a dog from lead pulling means the guardian has control, which sends an immediate message to the dog that he doesn't need to make decisions, and should another dog approach he doesn't need to worry about it, nor have feelings of either aggression or nervousness.

This doesn't mean that a dog cannot walk in front but he must wait for permission to go forward and not take it for granted that he can lead the way. A pack leader doesn't let his pack go in front and then keep asking it to come back; he

Barney is walking nicely on a lead and keeping calm past temptations such as livestock. The lead passes behind the handler and the hold on the lead is relaxed.

SHEPHERD'S COMMENT:

'We are our dogs' guardians and as such we protect them; in so doing we enable them to feel safe and they will be able to grow into confident dogs knowing that we will handle any problems that may arise.'

leads the way and any freedom to roam is permitted by him and not taken for granted. A parent doesn't allow a child to go ahead and meet strangers and make his own decisions; the child takes the lead from the parent, not the other way round.

There is a difference between dogs walking ahead on a loose lead and dogs pulling ahead. The dog on a loose lead is not taking control, unless he pulls the moment he sees another dog or a person he wants to approach, in which case he was only walking on a loose lead because at the time there was nothing of interest to make it worth taking control. This usually happens with an older dog, as a young dog will use his energy to pull on a lead simply because he hasn't learned how to conserve energy. A slightly older dog convinces his guardian he is being good, and saves his energy for when he sees something he believes it is worth pulling towards.

CONSEQUENCES OF LEAD PULLING

Dogs use their senses to determine how to deal with an approaching dog or person. Their sight and hearing provide them with some information, but their sense of smell will tell them everything they need to know. If a stranger is approaching and your dog is in front of you, he will be nearer to that stranger than you are and, as the distance between you reduces, the dog will begin picking up information about the person (or it may be an approaching dog) and decide how to react. He will see his reaction to the situation as being his decision to make because he was in front and taking control of the lead.

Rosie is in front, with her tail in a dominant position; her body is tense and she is threatening Rex. Rex's handler has him in a vulnerable position: he is not dominant, his tail is going down and he is turning away feeling very worried.

We can learn so much from a dog's body language. Rosie is a bully with other dogs. Here, she is leading the way, pulling her handler forwards while she sniffs the ground. The handler's shoulder is pulled forwards and the lead is across the front.

Rosie has been brought back into her handler's protective space, and her body is now more relaxed and she is calming down. Note the lead is now behind the handler and not in front. Rex has been moved into a more protected position and with Rosie's dominant energy blocked and relaxed, he is much happier.

The strong or over-confident dog

If he is a strong dog who likes to take control he may decide to growl at, or even try to fight, an approaching dog and this decision will be made quickly as he will not have the time to use his senses correctly, allowing him to make a positive judgement. With an approaching person, the dominant dog may be aggressive as soon as they get near enough. He will often begin by barking or growling a warning but if this doesn't work, and he thinks the person is going to walk into his space, he may allow him to come very close and then, with no warning, show his teeth with intent to bite.

The nervous or sensitive dog

The nervous dog will not be happy taking control, and when in front and pulling on a lead he will begin to panic if he feels intimidated. He will rarely want to approach, or be approached by, an unknown dog or person, and if he finds himself in that situation he will become very submissive and hope that he receives a friendly response. If the response, whether of friendly intent or not, makes him feel he is at risk, he will resort to nervous aggression and, like the more dominant dog, he will often appear as if he is going to accept a stroke from someone, but at the last minute will resort to nervous aggression in an attempt to protect himself.

The confident and friendly dog

If your dog is a friendly chap who loves everyone he sees he may not wait to pick up information from anyone approaching. He is probably going to move in for attention, wagging his tail, being friendly and trying to jump up, and if another dog is involved he may be just as enthusiastic without waiting to see if his attention is welcome. There is rarely a problem with this type of dog being aggressive as he loves everyone and firmly believes that everyone loves him. However, not everybody welcomes advances from other dogs and if this friendly lad approaches either a strong or a nervous dog there can be severe repercussions. The dominant dog will be more than happy to start a fight and the nervous dog will be terrified. There is also the possibility that the object of the confident dog's attention may be blind or deaf or very old, in which case there may be a very unhappy and annoyed guardian to placate. Not everyone loves dogs: some people are frightened of them and some are allergic to them and, just like dominant and nervous dogs, they will react accordingly. The friendly dog may easily find himself in such a situation, and if he is met with aggression he can soon become like the nervous and sensitive dog, resorting to nervous aggression to protect himself.

TAKING BACK CONTROL

Puppies follow their mother, the pack follows the leader and the leader takes control. If the leader is the family dog then he assumes control, but quite often he is doing what he has been taught to do, and if we look at the way we communicate from our dog's point of view, we can

As soon as Rex realized he was being looked after and protected when on a lead he learned to relax, happy to walk in front or at the side knowing that he could step backwards and be safe. The handler's body is relaxed and the hands are very gentle on the lead.

CASE HISTORY – LADDIE LEARNS TO LEAD WALK

Laddie trusted me and would follow me out of his pen into the garden and back in again. When he was introduced to a lead, any resistance was to lean back, not to pull forwards, but the important relationship that I had carefully built with him meant this lasted only for a few moments. He trusted me and was happy to follow where I went, on or off the lead, and because he trusted me he was equally happy to walk at my side, or a little behind if he saw a stranger, letting me deal with any problems that might arise. Laddie came into rescue at the age of ten months; he had seen little of the outside world and never had either a collar or a lead on but in less than three weeks he walked perfectly wearing an ordinary collar and lead! A lot of dogs who have become accustomed to a collar and lead from puppyhood start to pull the moment the lead goes on, usually because they have learned to pull and not been shown how to follow.

soon see how easily we can teach them to do the very thing we don't want. If the ground rules of standing back at the door and waiting to follow haven't been established, the young dog will start his walk feeling he is in control. You might know you are going to walk down the path and turn left, but if your dog is in front and pulling on a lead then he is taking you down the path and you are following him to the left!

The principle of lead walking remains the same for every type of temperament, but the method of lead walking must be adapted to complement that temperament. A nervous dog needs to feel protected for his own safety, a dominant dog has to be protected for the safety of others, and the friendly dog needs to be protected from the mistake of making unwelcome advances. Just as a dog feels he is in control if he is taking the lead, he will feel protected if you are taking the lead, so to be able to walk or stand in front of your dog while he is on a loose lead immediately gives you control over any situation that may arise, making the vulnerable dog feel safe and allowing the strong dog to let you manage any situation that may arise. But your dog must be content to let you take over, and this won't happen as long as he is pulling or taking the strain of the lead. Taking and keeping control isn't difficult if we Pause And Think of how we can make it easy for a dog to understand what we want. It is all too easy, without realizing it, to give them mixed and confusing messages.

MIXED MESSAGES

If a dog pulls in front and his handler drags him back, the dog is still pulling forwards until he reaches the handler's side, then he may hear a 'good dog' or 'heel' and he may receive a treat. But he is being praised for the overall action: he went in front, got dragged back and received praise. To get that praise or treat again his mind will tell him he needs to be in front and pulling. This isn't difficult for him – as he sees it this is something he is used to doing and he wants to do it; the fact that he gets pulled back every so often is an inconvenience but at least he gets praise or a treat for it. Add to this the fact that he will probably hear the words 'heel', 'close', or 'back' as he is being pulled back, but as his handler is pulling him back he is still pulling forwards, so whichever word he hears will be associated with pulling and not with walking easily on a lead. Remember, we need to persuade a dog to do what we want and then give the word we want him to associate with that action at the time he is doing it and not as we are trying to make him do it.

Once a dog has reached the end of the lead he will throw his neck and shoulders forward and-

TOP LEFT: *Barney is learning on a quiet road how to behave at the kerb. In this picture, although the lead is behind him, the handler is not paying him any attention and does not have him in a protected position. As a car approaches, Barney begins to show signs of stress by licking his lips.*

TOP RIGHT: *Here the handler has connected to Barney. He has taken him back from the edge of the road and put his leg across the front of him to tell him he is safe. Barney immediately begins to relax.*

LEFT: *Barney has progressed to a more built-up area. His handler is at the kerb edge with Barney behind him. He has connected with him before concentrating on the traffic, the lead is gentle and the body strong and Barney is happy to sit back and let him take control.*

put all his weight into pulling, often dragging his guardian towards the grass verge, where a variety of smells await him. But he could equally well be pulling towards another dog or person, which can cause panic both in his guardian and in the other people involved. He really needs to hear a calm and confident voice that he recognizes, but instead he will probably hear raised and anxious voices; this will raise his stress and excitement levels by sending him a message that everyone is joining in with him.

COLLARS AND LEADS

There is a variety of leads, harnesses and special collars to choose from but the connection between your hand and your dog is a very important one and can be compared to a parent holding a child's hand. A gentle squeeze can convey to the child a message of reassurance, confidence or even a reminder for good manners. Similarly any insecurity, or even over-confidence, a child may be experiencing will be communicated to the parent by pressure, release or the tiniest tremor in the child's hand. A dog doesn't have a hand for us to hold so we have to make sure that any connection we have is kind and sensitive to the dog's feelings. Special leads or harnesses can be purchased that are designed to make it easier to control a dog who pulls on a lead, but training a dog to walk correctly is a better solution than making it easier for the handler to hold him when he is pulling. If when a normal lead is re-applied the dog continues to pull, then he has not learned anything from the alternative method, and as long as he continues to pull, he is leading the way and in control. It is often considered that a lead attached to a collar can hurt a dog's throat, but this can only happen if the dog is pulling. By replacing the collar with a harness, the pressure goes on the chest and the shoulders, and similarly on anything that goes around the dog's head or nose. With a dog who doesn't pull, it doesn't matter what the lead is connected to, and if the lead is attached to a comfortable collar this allows him free rein to turn his head; if he decides to follow his gaze, the connection between your hand and the lead will alert you

to his intentions. This way he is not denied the freedom of any part of his body and you will be able to pick up messages through his lead of any mood changes he might be experiencing. Choose your lead carefully: too short a lead will restrict his freedom around your feet, and may make it difficult for you to teach him to lead walk correctly. Retractable leads can be a little clumsy for lead training and, because the hand is not in direct contact with the lead itself, important messages between handler and dog can be missed as there is no empathy passing down the lead from the hand to the dog.

Holding the lead

The way the lead is held can make a difference to your dog's behaviour. If you grip the lead tightly, you send messages to your dog of uncertainty and impatience. Experiment by rolling your hand into a fist; clench it tightly and you will feel the tension go up your arm and into your shoulder. In the same way the tension also passes down

Jill is tri-coloured with amber eyes. Here the handler's body has become tense, with the lead bunched in a tight grip and the fists clenched. The tension has transmitted down the lead to Jill, who has become just as tense and is ready to leap forwards.

Once the handler has relaxed the hands and arms, the tension goes and the body becomes less aggressive. The calm of the body is transmitted down the lead to Jill, who can also begin to relax.

the lead to your dog and he will become a mirror image of you; his body will cease to be relaxed and an unsettled dog will either panic or throw himself forwards to pull. As the tension in your arm spreads to the rest of your body, all communication between you and the dog is lost. He is committed to getting his own way and you are tense and anxious about how to get him back under control. A nice calm feel on the lead is needed, with a steady walking pace: too fast and he will think it's a race, which he will try to win. Slow is better than fast as it will both give your dog thinking time and allow you time to study his movements and his body language and build a relationship with him.

YOUR DOG'S SPACE

Providing your dog with his own area in your home, whether it's a Dog Den, a bed or a quiet corner, gives him security and a place to feel safe in, but when he goes out for a walk he only has you. Suddenly he is attached to you but with no real idea of where he should stand, and if he sees

a lot of open space ahead of him, it can either fill him with excitement or make him nervous. If he begins in front of you, he is in your space and you are in his protective position, and if he is at the side of you he has adopted the sharing position, but if you stand him behind you he is shielded by your body and he is in your protective position. You can now invite your dog to come forwards to your side and into your space. This movement and body language may seem simple but it will convey a message to your dog that, even though you are now outside, you are still his parent figure and in control, and he is safe with you. To understand our dogs we need to forget what we may be thinking and concentrate on how they will interpret what we are trying to teach them. Issuing verbal requests they may not really understand can cause confusion but with body language, which is how dogs communicate and express themselves, there are no mixed messages and this makes training much easier.

The key to teaching a dog is time and patience, and lead walking is no exception; it is one of the most important aspects of training, but it is often the one most overlooked and rushed. A person may be prepared to spend an hour teaching a dog to 'give a paw' but expects that same dog to learn how to walk on a lead when he is outside with a lot of distractions and at a fast walking pace. Dogs need time to absorb new information and the more distractions there are around them, the more time they will need and the harder it becomes for them to learn.

FIRST STEPS WITH AN EASY DOG

The first steps are the most important. Stand your dog behind you and hold the lead with both hands at your centre back. This position is important as he will soon learn that your hands behind your back means he stands behind you, but when they drop to your side he is invited forwards. Your body will now do the 'talking' to him. If you are tense he will be worried but if you relax he will feel safe. Don't stand like a statue – have your feet slightly apart, take a few deep breaths and be aware of your dog's stance; although your body needs to be relaxed it also

With a strong dog, one leg is back so he is a pace behind the front leg. Be patient and wait for your dog to connect with you, then move forwards and gently back again.

How to stand your dog behind you. It is important that you keep your hands together at centre back as this is a signal to your dog to come behind you (even when he's off the lead); when you drop your hands to your side he can come forwards. The body needs to be strong but gentle, with the feet slightly apart for balance. Notice how relaxed the hands are on the lead.

needs to be positive. If he tries to come to your side bring him gently back behind you, either with the lead or with a gentle movement of your body. Once he is relaxed, drop your hands to your side and walk forwards. He will automatically move forward to be at your side but if he tries to go too far in front then repeat the process before he gets to the end of the lead and starts pulling.

FIRST STEPS WITH A WILFUL DOG

With a strong or wilful dog, teaching him to walk correctly on a lead and not try to take control is important. If he feels he can lead or control the walk, he will believe he is also in control of other

When your dog gets it right and keeps connecting with you, don't be afraid to show affection. Bess's body is very relaxed and she's so pleased that she has got it right that she is asking for, and receiving, some quality reward time. Always start any training in a very quiet area. If you don't have anywhere suitable at home take your dog in the car to somewhere peaceful.

areas in his life, and a strong dog will take charge of any situation that may arise instead of looking to you for leadership.

Whatever your dog's temperament, all walks should begin the same way, with him standing behind you. The nervous dog will feel secure and the strong dog will understand he's not in control, but some dogs do resent not being the leader. Stand him behind you and if he jiggles from side to side make sure you bring him back behind you; it's a very easy mistake to keep moving to the side to stay in front of your dog, but he should be moving to be behind you, not you moving to try to keep in front of him. Making sure you don't tread on his feet, walk him backwards a few paces, still keeping him behind you, and then walk the same number of paces forwards. If you repeat this two or three times he will probably sit down and look at you to see if that is what you wanted. Tell him he's a good dog, drop your hands to your side and let him move forwards with you. If he speeds up and tries to go too far in front, bring him back behind you.

MOVING FORWARDS

Each dog is different and each handler needs to find the best method for their dog and then adapt it so that is comfortable for both of them. The three main points to remember before moving forwards are that the space in front of you is yours, the space behind you is your dog's, and permission has to be granted for your dog to move forwards into your space. It sounds very simple but a dog will always remember what he did first, so if the first lessons involve him going in front and pulling, he will assume that it is acceptable behaviour. Changing behaviour is never easy, so it's better to try to work as much as possible in a stress-free area that will help you. Your garden is a good place to start but even better is a hall-way, a path or a hedged or fenced track, ideally with as few distractions as possible. Putting the lead on in the house and standing in a room doorway, walking along a hall, going out of the front door, down the path and back again is the best way to begin, and you can do

When you take your dog in your car, make sure he is secure and use the opportunity to keep teaching him new things.

When your dog fully understands that he doesn't jump straight out of the car as soon as the door opens, then as he matures he will be content to relax and wait for your instructions.

it several times a day, once each time. After each short session make a fuss of your dog, but during each session keep your praise to a calm 'good dog'. If you are feeding him on a diet that is not too high in energy and have worked on keeping him calm, these lessons will be absorbed quickly. He will enjoy the interaction with you and it will give him plenty to think about, so will keep him mentally stimulated without being over-excited.

The process of standing him behind you and moving forwards a few steps is done very slowly, and when you drop your hands to your side to start your walk be careful not to move too quickly; your dog will understand you dropping your hands and the increased pace as a signal to move forwards but you don't want him to think it's a race. Each time he does what you want tell him what a good lad he is, still keeping your voice calm. If he moves forwards and doesn't attempt to pull, carry on and enjoy his companionship – but don't let him get so far in front that he can start pulling again and don't walk faster to keep up with him. Whenever your dog looks up at you, reward him with a smile, a gentle touch or a few calm words to help to create and maintain a strong bond between you.

If your dog is willing to listen and enjoys pleasing you, he will be happy to walk at your side. He will soon learn that with a loose lead he still gets to enjoy all the things he did when he was pulling, but he will feel both safer and more relaxed.

THE CONSTANT PULLER

There is no quick fix for any problem and a dog that is constantly pulling is rarely a pleasure to walk with, making it a temptation to let him off the lead to run free. However, a dog running free when he has already controlled the walk can create even more problems, as any wilfulness will make his recall unreliable. It is important that your dog still stands behind you for a few moments before moving forwards; without this, it's a little like telling a child to behave without first teaching them how to behave. Your dog needs to know that he walks at the side or in front of you because you want him to, not because he

Bess is a forward-going dog and likes to keep moving, so once she has learned how to stand behind her handler, the pace has been increased a little. The lead comes from behind to prevent Bess pulling the handler's body off-balance, and this way every six or seven strides she can be moved from the left to the right side, crossing behind the handler. This enables the pace to be increased but Bess is still under control.

Bess has been moved from behind the handler to the other side and sits down of her own accord when she realizes that pulling is not an option. Note how in both photographs there is no tension on the lead and the hands are relaxed, with attention fully on the dog and talking to her.

demands it. It is also important that you keep your hands together behind your back as the movement of your hands will 'tell' him when to be back and when he can come forwards. A dog will always observe your body movements but he won't always listen to your voice. The more he argues with you and the more you argue back, the less likely it is that he will take on board what you are trying to achieve, so teach him to stand calmly behind you in your home and in your garden, and if you block him with your body going out of the gate you will have achieved control at the start of the walk.

Your dog needs to listen to you rather than ignore you in favour of pulling, and if he doesn't do this voluntarily you need to make him constantly aware of your presence. To do this, keep making him change which side of you he is walking on as you are moving forwards but move him behind you and not in front of you. This needs to be done quickly and smoothly, so the lead should be long enough for him to walk at your side but short enough for you to be able to move him with the least effort and body movement. You may find it strange to begin with, but a gentle movement of your hands from side to side behind you and a little hip movement and you will find you can move forwards at a steady walking pace while your dog doesn't have time to sniff or look around. This method is not intended to wind him up, nor to enable you to walk faster 'swinging' him from side to side; it's a gentle movement and is only used at the start of the walk or for periods when he tries to revert back to being in control. Once he realizes that he isn't able to pull to get in front of you, he will settle to trotting behind or at your side. If you do it too quickly, a clever dog will soon begin to change sides on his own decision and not yours, so be aware of which side he decides he wants and change it. For example, if he tries to pull you to the left grass verge on a path, change him to the right side of you. This method cannot be used on a roadside as your dog needs to walk on your inside, away from any passing, or oncoming, vehicles. If there is a wall at the side of the pavement you can use it to help to keep your dog back, but if you walk your dog on your inside, away from the traffic, and hold the lead in the hand on the opposite side to your dog across the back of you, it will be easier to stop him pulling ahead and will allow you to walk a little faster to a quieter area.

WALKING ON A LOOSE LEAD

One of the most important things to remember is that you never let your dog take up the pull on the lead. Apart from the fact that this puts him in control, it will take away your balance and pull your arm forwards, making it difficult for you to regain control. One of the disadvantages of a retractable lead is that a dog with a tendency to pull doesn't have a set boundary at the end of a lead, as each time he wants to go further the lead is extended, allowing him to dictate his own boundary. For training purposes it is better to have a normal dog lead and a longer training line. When on the lead your dog has less space to pull into and the change from the short to the longer line will indicate to your dog that you have given him more freedom. This will reap benefits when teaching the recall.

If your dog is walking correctly, the lead should be loose and any tension should be taken up by you. For example, by very gently taking up the slack on the lead you are able to send a message to your dog that you want his attention. The benefit for you is a dog that is joy to walk with and the benefit for the dog is being able to feel comfortable without any gadgets and knowing he has a direct link to you. When a dog gets to the end of the lead and feels the tension he will take over, throwing his weight forwards into pulling; at this point your arm and body are brought forward and you lose your balance. Before he gets far enough forward to be able to take control of the lead, you must take up the slack; this is done without jerking or tugging, and there are several ways of doing so, depending on your dog and which is the easiest for you both.

Before your dog gets to the end of the lead, bring your weight back into your shoulder; this will bring the balance back into your favour and, instead of him pulling and thinking he is in control, you will be sending a message to him not to try to take control. With this method you are

Tess is in a busy built-up area but she is totally relaxed. Her handler is a step back from the edge of the kerb with her right leg ready to move across the front of Tess should she feel the slightest tension in the lead, which is behind her back. Tess is not made to feel vulnerable by the traffic, and motorists can see she is relaxed and not looking to chase into the road.

REACHING THE END OF THE LEAD

The dog's view:
He has reached the end of the lead, which is preventing him from doing as he pleases, but it doesn't pose a problem as long as he can throw his weight forwards like a sled dog and just keep pulling. He is happy to pull as eventually he will get to where he wants to be, and whoever is on the other end of the lead will be dragged along with him. He may have to suffer the inconvenience of being dragged back by the handler every so often but then he gets told he's a good boy so all is well in his world.

The handler's view:
If the dog is repeatedly pulled back he will eventually understand that he shouldn't go forwards and pull, especially if he gets a reward every so often for being dragged back. If he doesn't pick up this message then he is either desperate for a run or there is a need to find a way of making pulling him back easier.

The last thing you want is a dog who pulls. You can see the difference in the balance of the handler's body between this photograph and the first picture in this chapter. By not allowing the upper arm to go forwards the handler is not only keeping balanced but is preventing the dog from leaning forwards into his shoulders.

taking charge and making sure your dog doesn't get to the end of the lead and pull. You do need to make sure that this doesn't become an exercise that is repeated throughout the entire walk, as it will become another form of game to your dog of how to take control. Another method is to stop your dog but keep walking past him; this way, instead of trying to bring him back, you are overtaking him. Some dogs pick this up very quickly as they hear the praise of 'good dog' when you are in front; there is no tugging or pulling, he simply stands and allows you to walk past him and take control.

KEEPING YOUR DOG FOCUSED ON YOU

Changing direction will keep your dog's attention on you, but not if he is in front of you. Once in front he is in the lead and when you turn to go the other way he has to speed up to overtake you; if, at that point, you change direction again he will soon think it's a great game. Instead, change direction while he is behind you, at your side or slightly in front of you and don't turn to walk in a straight line as he will soon begin to anticipate your movement and beat you to it. Find a nice quiet area in a reasonably open space - perhaps a yard, a small field, a quiet car park or an open space along your favourite walk – and spend a few moments walking slowly in circles, figure eights and half figure eights (a letter S). Your dog should be on a loose lead and his attention will be on you because each time he thinks he might take control by going in front you change direction but as he never knows which way you are going to turn he has to keep focused on you. While doing this exercise keep your body very relaxed with a gentle hold on the lead and it will soon become one of your dog's favourite interactions – and it's more productive than throwing a ball.

SUMMARY

If your dog pulls on the lead, he is controlling the walk. This means he will also try to take control of any situation that may arise on the walk.

If you grip the lead tightly it will send a message down the lead to the dog of a lack of confidence, which can make him nervous or overconfident. This will make both of you tense for different reasons.

If your dog is constantly sniffing when on a walk, he is paying attention to the smells left by other dogs and not to you. You need him to want to keep his attention on you of his own free will and to walk with you without pulling and with just an ordinary collar and lead.

METHODS

Start every walk with your dog following you, not pulling, and keep a gentle feel on the lead. Resist the urge to give your dog a command if this might give him a mixed message. You might intend 'heel' or 'back' to mean he has to walk at your side, but if he hears it when he's being pulled back he will associate it with pulling.

When your dog is in front of you, don't let him take up the pull on the lead. By keeping him on a loose lead and his attention on you he will be more comfortable and it will help you to form a companionable relationship with him.

When teaching your dog to lead walk, it's better to have your lead running from hand to hand in a secure position so that your dog can't pull your shoulder forwards, which will put you off balance.

CASE HISTORY – BONNIE'S TRAINING

When Bonnie came into rescue at nine months old she not only pulled on a lead but constantly jumped up, getting herself so wound up that she couldn't stop yapping. Bonnie was so hyperactive and so stressed that trying to walk her behind was impossible. We adjusted her diet to start the calming process and in each training session her handler stood quietly with Bonnie behind her for a few moments. The instant Bonnie stood calmly they moved forwards and Bonnie could be quietly praised, even though the achievement of calm only lasted for a few seconds. Bonnie was young, with a short concentration span, and was making no effort to connect with her handler, so instead of going through the process of lead walking and progressing to a loose lead, which we knew would be a struggle, we started with her behind and then skipped forward to the circling and figure eight method. Within two days of short training sessions using this method Bonnie began keeping her attention on her handler, finding it fun trying to keep up with her movements. After three days we introduced the lead walking method of standing at the back and then moving to the side followed by her favourite 'which way next' game. Her walks became a variety of the different methods, all of which achieved the same results, and after two weeks she was a changed dog. She walked nicely on a lead, she loved her interaction figure eights and circles, which was fun for her but was done very calmly so she was thinking rather than getting excited, and she became totally focused on her handler. Bonnie's training was done in a very quiet area and she still had a long way to go after the first two weeks. It took almost another month before she could be just as calm when walking where there were more distractions, but she was not only much better behaved but also a far more relaxed and happy dog.

8 TEACHING THE RECALL

Teaching a dog to come back when called shouldn't be an issue: the bond between a dog and his guardian should be so strong that the dog will never want to be far away. However, the giving of mixed messages, and leaving training until after a dog has learned bad habits, may not only cause confusion but actually endorse the dog ignoring, or misinterpreting, the recall command.

WITH A PUPPY

With a puppy the recall is easy to teach: he will rarely be far away from his guardian and will frequently run back to maintain the connection with his parent figure. This usually only happens in the first few days, and it's a golden training opportunity that is not to be missed. Each time he comes running back to you make sure he hears you give him his recall; it is not a 'command', it is a welcoming tone, and when he has covered the short distance to you don't let him trot off again straight away; instead stroke him and make a fuss of him, giving him every reason to want to be with you. Once he begins to feel more confident, he will start to push his boundaries – and not coming back when he hears you call will be on his list of things to try. When this happens, don't

Every dog lover's worst nightmare is seeing your dog running at full speed away from you and knowing he will not come back when you call. From the first day your new dog or puppy comes into your life encourage him always to come to you when you call him.

keep repeating his recall; go to him and gently take him back to the spot where you called him from. Remember that because you only called him once, he only ignored you once, and maybe you were not attentive enough at the time to realize that he was not going to come back to you. Dogs will rarely do something without giving notice of their intentions, and if we fail to pick up the message then we are at least partly responsible for their actions. He may have been intent on sniffing something, or pricked his ears and been concentrating on something he could see in front; as a puppy his concentration on you will soon be diverted, so it is up to you to teach him to always be aware of you and to keep tuning in to your voice. When you have him back at the point where you originally called him from, stroke him so that he settles down to sit with you and make sure you don't let him go again without a lead on. Stroking at this point is not rewarding bad behaviour as you have taken him back to the place where you called him from; you have shown him what he should have done when you called him and, although you have had to help him do it, he is only a pup and will constantly be in need of your guidance. What you must remember is how and why it happened. He was feeling over-confident and you didn't spot the signals, so he now goes on a long lead or training line until both you and he have re-established a good rapport. The little bit of extra thought and effort this takes on the first occasion when he thinks he doesn't always have to come back to you will save a lot of frustration and training time when he reaches adolescence and thinks not coming back is acceptable behaviour.

WITH AN ADOLESCENT OR OLDER DOG

Adolescence is the transition between puppy and adult dog, when all the boundaries that were taught in puppyhood are tested and pushed, before finally settling to a calmer adult way of life. It can begin as early as six months and can last until a dog is two years old, and if a young dog goes into adolescence with existing

A happy recall. There can be no better feeling than when your dog runs to you with so much love and enthusiasm, but always make sure the first time you let him off the long line that you are in a fenced area.

In an area where there are no fences or other restrictions, and where the foliage can easily hide a dog, you need to be confident that your dog will still come running to you if he is off lead.

problems it will take him longer to mature. The older dog with a poor recall will have spent all his life habitually ignoring all requests to come back, and it will have become a way of life for him. This makes it more difficult to train him but by working on the bond between you of love, respect and lead walking he will soon learn that you are worth giving up all the wonderful ground scents that freedom may bring and will come bounding back to you.

THE HAPPY RECALL

A recall should be happy and your dog should really want to be with you. Returning to you for a toy is different from returning because he has heard his recall. If he is coming back purely for a treat or a toy he is not coming back to you, he is coming back for whatever you are offering in exchange for his return. But what would happen if you didn't have something to offer, or if he were frightened and his fear outweighed the lure of the treat or the toy? Playing with a ball and enjoying a game is different from a dog coming back to be with you because you have called him. Think how bad-mannered it would be considered if a parent called their child but was ignored because the child was too busy playing with a friend, digging in a sandpit or just playing and couldn't be bothered to acknowledge that they were being called. It isn't any different for a dog and there may come a time when that instant recall can save a dog's life.

When a child ignores a parent he can be considered to be bad-mannered, but a similar scenario with a dog is often dismissed as not being a problem because 'the dog doesn't understand'. But dogs can understand if it's made very clear what is wanted of them, so it is up to us to make sure that we do not give them mixed messages.

WHAT THE RECALL SHOULD MEAN

The recall is the word or words used to call your dog back to you, but he may not always interpret it that way. If your dog is running in front with his back to you he is thinking forwards, so when he hears the words that are intended to be his recall, the association is with the action of running from and not to you. When your dog is actually on his way back to you, and really wanting to be with you, that is the time he should hear the words you want him to associate with that action. If you keep repeating your recall command, you are telling your dog that he doesn't need to respond the first time, and each time you do repeat it your tone will be different as

HOPE'S RECALL

I was walking with six-year-old Hope along a quiet path in an unfamiliar area. At the start of the walk I reminded Hope to keep behind me until I gave him permission to walk at my side, finally letting him off his lead to trot on ahead. Hope was several yards in front when he suddenly swerved off to the right on a path going into a small wood, and the child within me thought it would be great to explore – so instead of calling him back I followed him. He was never far in front and was in my sight the entire time, so I was able to see the danger he was about to step into. He turned left and a few short paces in front of him was a railway line; the only thing between Hope and the railway was a broken fence. I called his name gently, and he turned and looked at me, and when I called him back he came running to me for his usual hug and cuddle. The outcome could have been so different had he not loved coming back when he was called, if my voice had registered panic or if I hadn't gone through the golden rules of walking him first behind me, and then with me, to remind him that we were in a new area and I was the one in control.

Buddy didn't want to run off but he did like to run around before coming back. He has a long line on him and his handler has tilted her body slightly to one side to stop him from jumping up or coming directly to the front of her.

teaches him, so it is not a new concept for him – but it is one that he will ignore if you let him.

THE RECALL SOUND

You can teach your dog to come back to you with practically any word or words you choose, but whatever you choose it must be interesting and something that your dog will not struggle to hear, and ideally something that is not too easy for him to ignore. Try to avoid the temptation of including his name in the recall, and it's better to use at least two syllables to help to make it a lyrical sound. If you use his name with every request or command his name will become part of that sound, and as he knows his name it will also be the first thing he will recognize,

As soon as he is in the protected position, Buddy's handler brings him to her side to let him know how pleased she is with him.

you get a little more stressed and a little more determined. So the recall you want your dog to return to has suddenly become louder and more intense, making it a totally different sound from the one you started with and from the one you will give next time you call him. The recall should never be dismissed as something that can be taught at a later date or when your dog is a little older. It is essential that your dog comes back to you when you call him and that he understands that he must come at the first time of asking. It is one of the four non-negotiable commands that nature makes him aware of and his mother

If there is a problem that upsets a dog, he needs to know to recall to the protected position. Once Buddy learned the body language that meant he went into that safe position, he began to learn his more casual recall.

he doesn't come to you, it could be because he didn't hear you the first time, or didn't understand what you wanted, but it's also possible that he didn't have a fair chance to do as you asked. A dog's hearing is different from ours: whereas we can hear several sounds at once, and even give them equal importance, a dog will only hear what he is really focused on. His sight, sense of smell and his hearing will all target the same thing, so if something comes into his range that he finds interesting, all his senses will divert to it. His sight will be focused on his target but the first you may know of it will perhaps be his ears pricking up, and by that point you have lost his attention, because his sense of hearing has left you and teamed up with his other senses and all his focus is on whatever is ahead. Seeing the world ahead through your dog's senses helps you to understand the need for two things: to keep your dog's hearing tuned in to the sound of your voice, and to maintain a vigilant lookout so you can divert his attention before his ears go up and he becomes focused on something other than you.

Using your dog's name as a 'notice to recall' will make it easier for him to do as you ask, and will avoid you having to repeat the recall command. He will be used to hearing his name and therefore he is more likely to tune in to that sound, and it is already in his memory in varying tones and volumes. Instead of following his name immediately with his recall, allow him to respond to his name first by looking at you and then waiting to see what you want of him. When his attention has come to you and away from anything that may be in front, you can then give him the recall. You are using two of the four natural and non-negotiable commands (Chapter 5) that he will have understood from his mother. When she called to her brood she expected their attention immediately, and once it was given to her she would then decide whether to call them back or let them carry on. But it would be her choice and she would remain in control. When he has responded to his name and given you his attention, his focus is back on you, making it much easier to give him the recall, but if it is a stilted one-syllable word it will not be a very

making it easy for him to ignore the next part of the sound.

Look at it for a moment from your dog's perspective. He regularly hears his name and when he does it comes before various other instructions, some of which he will respond to and some he may be less keen to take notice of. Because it is used regularly he will usually always respond to his name, but not necessarily to what follows it, particularly if he is at a distance from you. Instead of using his name as a prefix to his recall, use it as a 'notice to recall'. If you call him back and welcoming sound to him. If you summoned a small child with the word 'Come', it would sound harsh and unfriendly and if shouted over a distance it could be quite intimidating, and it has just the same effect on a dog, which is why it is often a temptation to prefix the request with the dog's name.

You are commanding your dog to come back to you and you expect him to obey; in that respect it is a command, or an order, but if issued in that manner you are more likely to alienate him. At the other extreme, however, if you go overboard with a high-pitched voice and your hands waving in the air he is less likely to think it is not negotiable and more likely to respond to it as a game. This may seem fine, but if he chooses not to play and instead to keep his focus on another dog or a person then his behaviour cannot be considered as being disobedient, as he is merely stating that he doesn't want to play a game with you at that moment. He needs to hear something he is used to tuning in to, which is his name, and then for a happy recall he needs a positive and happy sound, such as 'here to me', 'come to me', 'come back here', or any three sounds you choose. The words are unimportant but the sound of them is everything for a good recall: the words are rolled into one 'here-to-me', spoken in your normal voice (he does know your voice but he won't know a high-pitched or over-excited tone) and in a nice rhythm.

Whether the recall is a casual one or a protected one, Buddy enjoys some quality time each time he's recalled, making him want to stay rather than run off.

THREE LITTLE QUESTIONS

If your dog appears to be ignoring you, ask yourself three things: did he understand the command you gave him? Was it delivered correctly and was it in context? If the answer to only one of those is 'no', the dog is not entirely at fault. For example, during training if a dog doesn't fully understand the recall, he won't respond to it. If the recall is delivered in a stressed voice or one of a different pitch he won't respond to it. If the recall is given repeatedly for no reason and no joy of returning for some quality time he won't respond to it.

It is very rare that all three questions with the recall, or any other command, are answered with a 'yes', enabling the handler to be able to say that the dog is at fault. Even if only one answer is 'no' and two are 'yes', the dog still cannot be accused of not responding.

TEACHING THE RECALL

Don't wait until your dog is at a distance from you to teach him the recall. If he doesn't know what you mean, he has no reason to come back when you call him. Begin at home by letting him hear the sound each time he comes to you of his own free will; there doesn't need to be a strict training regime and if an issue is made of teaching the recall there is a risk he will begin to challenge you and be defiant. Invest in a training line approximately 10 metres long (for the purpose of training it needs to be a suitably strong line similar to your lead but not a retractable one), and take it with you on your walk.

When you are lead walking your dog, you can prepare him for the recall by occasionally stopping and calling his name to get his focus on you, then intermittently calling him back to you for some special attention. Don't bring him back every time as your main objective is to get him

to respond to your request for focus. Never overload your dog with information; he needs time digest everything at his own pace.

When you reach a suitable place on your walk to let your dog go further, exchange the normal lead for the long line and carry on walking, letting him drift further away from you. Keep your eyes peeled so that before he sees something he can focus on you give him the 'notice to recall' using his name; if he doesn't respond, use the long line to turn him to face you. Once he is facing you, give him his recall (remember you have been teaching this request at home and on a walk

When a dog pulls on a short lead it can pull the handler off-balance, but on a long line the handler can be pulled over. Rex is a strong dog and cannot be trusted off the long line. In this picture you can see how the handler is being pulled forwards, while Rex is giving no sign of stopping.

With one hand trying to keep hold of the lead, the handler is struggling to regain balance.

on a short lead); wait a few seconds and if he doesn't respond, bring him to you with the line. When he gets to you, don't be in a rush to let him go again. Your dog's recall should be happy because he wants to be with you – not because you are offering treats and toys but because you have such a brilliant relationship that he rarely wants to be far from you. Sit with him for a few moments and spend some quality time with him, then if you wish you could give him a treat as you will be rewarding him for spending time with you and not for coming back only to rush off again. But be careful as your dog will soon know he gets a treat and will try to cut out the bonding time in favour of the titbit – and this is the last thing you want him to do.

TEACHING THE RECALL TO AN OVER-ACTIVE DOG

Training a dog is not difficult if the dog is receptive and willing to focus on you. If your dog has so much energy that he just refuses to listen to you, or doesn't seem able to stay still long enough to listen to what you are asking, then you need to let him expend some of that energy, but without compromising who is in control. The first thing to do is to check his diet to see if changing it can help to reduce his excess energy, and work on his lead walking for his focus before you begin teaching the recall. If you have a garden with a large lawned area you can begin your training there; if not, choose a quiet area within a short walking distance. If you don't have access to such an area locally and he is so full of mischief that it is difficult to lead walk him until he has used some of his excess energy, you may find it easier to take him in your car to a suitable place. Wherever you choose, it needs to be somewhere quiet and without too many distractions.

It doesn't matter how obstinate the dog is, you must take control of the walk and he needs to show some good manners both coming out of your home and getting out of your car. Make

Finally the handler is regaining composure but Rex's tail is flying high and he is still in control of the long line. Were he to set off again, the whole episode would be replayed and Rex might break free.

him stand for a second behind you and then walk with him at your side (or he can be slightly in front, but don't let him take up the pull on the lead). As soon as you are in an area where he can have more space to run, change the lead for the long training line but don't let him run to the full length of the line. Start with him on just half the line distance, and before he gets to the end of it use the line to turn him so that instead of running away from you he has been turned to run across the front of you. Keep repeating this until your dog is actually running at a steady pace in a circle around you (if you are familiar with horses, it is comparable to lunge-line training); to begin with you may need to move in a large circle yourself until he gets used to the idea, although most dogs pick this up very quickly. Don't let your dog think this is a game where he can do as he pleases; he needs to enjoy what he is doing, and he will if he receives plenty of praise for it, but he also needs to have a sense of achievement, something

he is concentrating on and working at. This is all part of his training and education but instead of allowing him thinking time, which he will use to his advantage, you are letting him work off some of his excess energy and at the same time you are teaching him how to keep some of his focus on you. When your dog is going round you in large circles at a steady pace (and not racing round), he not only has one ear in your direction but he can see you. Even if he doesn't appear to be looking at you he will be aware of any movement you make and as you move around inside the circle, not allowing him to face away from you and tug on the line, he will begin to enjoy trying to work out which way you are going to move next. This exercise is only a short one and it is not intended either to tire your dog out or to over-excite him; the purpose is to use up a little of his excess energy while he is learning to stay within your circle and to keep focused on you.

Because Rex is so strong-willed he needs to learn to circle, so that he will always have some visual contact with his handler. But he is still facing forwards and the handler's left hand is clenched, which sends a message down the line to Rex about how tense she is.

AVOIDING SETBACKS

Patience and perseverance are essential when teaching the recall, for it not only gives you control over your dog at a distance, but is also the lifeline that could prevent an accident. There is no such thing as a guaranteed recall: a dog is a dog and sometimes the smell of a rabbit or the sight of another dog running may make your dog ignore your call. It may only be momentary, but it can be a powerful reminder that the 100 per cent recall you thought you had is actually only 99 per cent.

When your dog comes back to you, don't stop him directly in front of you; teach him to come either behind you or to your side. Any more formal training with him sitting directly in front and looking up at you can come later, but at the start of your training you are teaching him not only good manners but also that you are his protector. If your dog comes back to you and sits facing you he has his back to anything that may seem like a problem to him, and not every walk can be guaranteed to be problem-free. If a much larger and/or dominant dog suddenly appears and exhibits threatening behaviour, your dog should want to come back to you and let you look after him, but if he has to sit with his back to the other dog he will feel very vulnerable. Another very good reason for asking your dog to come behind you before coming to your side means

SHEPHERD'S COMMENT:

'To get a 100 per cent performance away from home you need to be getting 200 per cent at home, and should you achieve it put at least 1 per cent down to Lady Luck, because with dogs and humans mistakes are inevitable.'

The handler's body is relaxed, the hands are gentle so the line has no tension and Rex is hearing a soft, calm voice. He has turned and is ready to move across the front of his handler rather than move away.

that his recall is not complete until he has passed behind your legs, which will reduce the chance of him stopping short before he gets to you. Some dogs begin with a good recall but it becomes less consistent as they are rewarded for coming back before they actually get to their guardian; they receive a quick 'good dog' or a treat and then run free again. Make sure that each time your dog returns you spend some time with him before letting him go again. If he comes back to you and receives a treat and then runs free again, in his mind he is returning only for the treat. If you spend time with him talking to him and stroking him, it is in his mind that he wants to be with you.

It can be very tempting to 'test' your dog's recall by taking off the long line too soon, which could result in all of your training suffering a set-back that may take weeks to resolve. You need to let your dog off the long line in stages rather than suddenly discarding it. You must be abso-

lutely certain that your dog understands and will respond to the recall, and you won't know that until you let him have a little more freedom. If your dog comes back to you in the garden or a fenced area without any hesitation then he is ready for the next step, but remember that what he can do when there are no distractions may be a different matter when there are. To begin with let the line trail rather than hold it, and if you have taught your dog to go in large circles rather than in a straight line you will always be able to take hold of the line again. Rather than wait until your dog's recall will be tested on a walk with something you can't control, try to stage a distraction by asking a friend to walk past with their dog. If your dog's recall isn't as good as you thought, your friend should stand and wait while you get him back under control. Don't wait until your dog is nearer to the distraction than he is to you, as a dog will always be tempted to react to what is nearest to him. If the distraction is 100

CASE HISTORY – DIGBY THE DEAF DOG

Being deaf, Digby's communication for his training was done mainly with body language and hand signals, but when he had his back to me and couldn't see what I was doing, I was aware that he could lose all contact with me. Digby was always on a 10-metre training line when we were out for a walk, but as far as he was concerned he never went more than 9 metres away from me, as that was the distance where I took control of the line and I never allowed him to take up the pull on it. One evening we were out for a long walk on the edge of dark when I realized that, although Digby was moving further away from me at a steady lope, the line was still on the ground. The catch on the line had been faulty and he was now running at a steady pace towards a main road. Shouting for him was no good and, although he was only going at a steady loping pace, I was no match for catching him up. Part of all our walks included me giving a very gentle tug on the line at 9 metres; Digby would stop and look round at me, and I would give him either a thumbs up for a good lad or signal him to come back to me. At exactly 9 metres away Digby stopped and looked round at me. I have never been as grateful for the time and commitment I have put in to communicating with my dogs as I was that evening as he came running back to me as soon as I gave him the signal.

Digby is deaf and all communication with him is via body language. Far from hindering any relationship, Digby loves communicating and learning new things.

metres away, then you need to take control of your dog before 50 metres, and the nearer he gets to the halfway line the less control you will have. Once he crosses the halfway line you may struggle even when he has a good recall, and your dog may not be able to resist the temptation to keep going when his natural instinct will be telling him that he is inside the fight or flight distance of the distraction.

A QUIET RECALL

When your dog is near you, call him in a soft, quiet voice, and make sure he comes to you by keeping his lead on if you have any doubt of his intention of doing as you ask. If you train him quietly he will acknowledge a normal voice when he is at a distance from you and shouting will be something you rarely need to do. To encourage your dog to listen to your calm voice, you need to keep your body language equally calm: waving your arms around and jumping up and down is the equivalent of shouting. The very fact that you love your dog and want him with you will change your body language from demanding to inviting, which will send him a message making him want to be with you. But sharp or erratic movements will produce a similar reaction from him, so that instead of coming back to you with the intention of being calm and staying with you, he will return wound up and raring to go again, which will tempt him to stop short on his recall.

SUMMARY

The importance of a good recall should never be undervalued. A dog who doesn't come back can harass other dogs and can even cause, or have, an accident.

When your dog is at a distance away from you and focused on something ahead of him, his hearing, like his other senses, will be tuned in to the object of his focus and he genuinely won't hear you.

Constantly recalling your dog and then letting him run free again straight away will tempt him to stop short on the recall and not come right back to you.

METHODS

Before teaching the recall make sure your dog walks well on a lead. Always start each lesson with him standing behind you or at your side on a loose lead for a few seconds before letting him run forwards.

Never try to teach the recall in a large area and without a long training line on your dog, and begin each session with just a short distance and a quiet voice.

When your dog comes back to you spend time with him so that he would rather stay with you than leave you, and when he is running keep him in a large circle so that his focus doesn't leave you.

9 LIVING WITH A RESCUE OR A PROBLEM DOG

Choosing a rescue dog isn't easy and you must make sure that the heart doesn't rule the head. It's no good taking a very nervous dog into a busy home, and a young, very energetic dog could prove too much for someone who leads a quiet life and doesn't want to have to brave the elements every day come rain or shine. When you go to a rescue centre and look at all the dogs needing homes, it isn't always easy to accept that you can only take one home with you, so before you start your search do a little bit of homework about the centre you are visiting.

FINDING YOUR RESCUE DOG

A good rescue centre will want to know about your home life, your expectations for your dog, your experience, your work or volunteer commitments and what type of home and garden you have. With the information you give them, they will know if they have a dog, or dogs, that may be suitable for you to choose from. Preferably they will bring any suitable dogs to you, rather than have you walk past rows of pens with dogs jumping up and barking, which not only stresses the dogs but may upset you if you see several dogs that you like, only to be told later that none of them is suitable.

The first meeting is very important. Although you know that you are about to offer a permanent and loving home to a dog, to the dog you are a total stranger. The only familiar face to the dog is the person bringing him to you. If you think about it, you wouldn't hand your dog over to a total stranger: it would almost feel like a betrayal – yet here is this dog, with the only person he knows and feels he can trust, being handed over to someone he has never seen in his life before. Give him time to get used to you and to want to come to you; don't walk straight up to him or stare at him. Try to think of him as a small child: he isn't one, of course, but he will have the same fears and anxieties. Some dogs may come bounding over to you without a care in the world, but in most cases a dog in a rescue centre is one in need of very careful and gentle introductions.

Be prepared to find that the type of dog you thought you wanted might not be the type of

Whether in a confined space or not, never approach an unknown dog from the front. He needs time to check you out and space to feel he can move away if needed. Approach from the side and stand sideways on to the dog, extending a hand so he can find out more about you. The handler has moved back but has the lead under her right foot so the dog cannot jump up and startle the person approaching.

The dog has connected with the handler and is relaxed enough to let the person approaching make contact. The handler still has her foot on the lead keeping everything calm, but no pressure is being put on the dog and there nothing directly in front of him so he has a feeling of space.

dog that you finally choose; there is no telling which dog is going to get into your heart, but at the same time don't offer a home to a dog just because he needs one. You will know deep down if the dog is the one that you can take home and love unconditionally; if you have any doubts don't make an immediate decision. Instead, go home and have a really good think about it. It's a huge commitment taking a dog into your home. Every dog needs stability and lots of love as a puppy, but a rescue dog may come to you with anxieties and problems inherited from his past and for the first few weeks, or even months, you may find you are struggling to build the relationship you had hoped for, but with patience and perseverance it will come. It takes at least three weeks to be able to assess a dog so before making your final decision ask how long the dog has

been in the rescue centre. If you have chosen a dog who has gone into rescue from a private home, the centre staff know all about his background and if there are no serious existing problems or issues, he should be able to be rehomed almost straight away. But if the dog came from a dog pound there will be no history with him and, prior to going into rescue, he will have spent at least seven days in a dog pound before travelling to the rescue centre, where he will have had to begin trying to get settled all over again. In addition to getting over the trauma of going from dog pound to rescue centre, the reason why he was in the pound in the first place can be a mystery until his story begins to unfold, and that can only happen with time. So if the dog you want to take into your life has arrived at the kennels from a dog pound and has only been in the care of the staff for a few days rather than a few weeks, any assessment made about his character in that short time may be inaccurate. So when choosing a rescue dog, make sure you are adopting from kennels that can give you as much information as possible about the dog, provided either by his previous family or based on a reasonably long-term assessment by the staff.

BEDS AND ESSENTIALS

If your chosen dog is well adjusted, with no issues or behavioural problems, he may just move in with you as if he's been there all his life, or he may be just a little on the bossy side and think he can take over your home, but in many cases rescue dogs are nervous and insecure, and would rather hide in your house than try to take it over. Whichever character type your dog fits into, it is better to begin to introduce him to your home, life and rules slowly, the first two types of dog because you don't want him to take over and the latter because you want him to finally feel safe and secure in his life.

Bringing a rescue dog into your home for the first time is a little bit like new baby syndrome – you want to rush out and buy everything you may possibly need, but for the first few weeks you need to find out what your dog wants and not what you think he might want. If he's a nerv-

Don't be in a rush to take your dog out for a walk too soon. A nervous dog will benefit from you spending time just getting to know him; if you're outside, even in your garden, make sure you keep a lead on him.

ous dog toys may frighten him, and if he's a bold lad with a bit of attitude he may think you have provided them for him to chew. A dog will tell you all about his past if you allow him the time to do so. By taking note of anything he is frightened of and how he behaves at certain times or in certain situations, you will be able to work out what kind of a life he may have had previously. But don't jump to conclusions too quickly: a lot of small, fine-boned Collies can be nervous of their own shadow and often appear to have been abused when in fact they have been misunderstood.

Before collecting your dog from the rescue centre take a good look around your home and choose the quietest and calmest area for your dog's bed. Be prepared to provide a Dog Den (indoor kennel) if he needs one so he has a place of his own to retreat to and to feel safe in. You will need a lead of reasonable length (if he is a nervous dog don't get a retractable one, as the noise when it retracts may scare him) and a long training line such as the one used for teaching the recall. Whatever kind of bed you prefer, it may be better to have a vet bed or soft mattress in his Dog Den and the same in a plastic bed to begin

THE IMPORTANCE OF PATIENCE

If you took a foster child into your family, you would not give them immediate access to everything in the home. They would go to their room to unpack, settle in and then begin to learn how the family works and what the house rules are. The same principle applies when you take a rescue dog into your home. It is a new way of life for him and for the first few days he is in a home with people he doesn't know, voices he isn't used to and an area where he has never been before, and he doesn't know where he should or should not be. He has a lot to learn in just settling in and most dogs will be happy to be given time to learn by observation. The most precious gift you can give your dog is patience and time to adjust while gently guiding him through what will be his boundaries.

with; choosing a very thick spongy bed may cause problems if he has any night 'accidents' for the first week as you need something which is quick to wash and easy to dry. Provide more than one bed for him so he can have one in a calm area for night and 'down' time (this would be his Dog Den), and a bed in the sitting room or kitchen so he has a place of his own to sit in when he is with you.

SETTLING IN

When your dog comes to you from the rescue centre he will leave behind all he knows, so take a small, soft blanket for him to sit on in your car. By the time you get him home his scent will be on the blanket, which will provide him with something familiar and comforting in his bed. As exciting as it may be finally having your dog at home with you, he needs some peace and quiet, so keep visitors to a minimum and for the first few days try to keep to just family only in the home. Everything that you are doing you have had time to think about and to prepare for, but from your dog's point of view it is completely unexpected. He has gone from a kennel environment with other dogs, a routine and a lot of barking around him to being in a home, with the sound of washing machines, telephones, televisions and other household gadgets, which he may not have heard before. There will be no routine that he understands and nothing at all familiar apart from the blanket you have given him and his name; it might not be the name you would have chosen but it is his and he will be used to it, so allow him to keep that one piece of familiarity as he will have enough to learn without adding a new name to the list.

In the first few days start as you would with a puppy. Assume your dog doesn't understand anything and start with the very basics. This way you will soon find out what he already knows and won't make the mistake of trying to persuade him to do something he doesn't understand. What he does on day one will stay with him. You may want to show him around your home, walk him round the garden and maybe take a little stroll down the road to the park. But if you do this,

in his mind he will see everything you show him as his boundaries. He has gone overnight from having a pen in a rescue centre to having the home, the garden and down the road as far as the park. He only knows what he is shown and if, on the first day, he is given a boundary of half a mile away then that is where he will go to if a door or a gate is left open. He needs to know what is his home and garden, and anything else is better left for at least another few days until he is settled in and feeling a little more confident.

Before letting any dog loose in the garden, even with a long line on, check that your fences are as dog-proof as you can make them – remembering that dogs don't just jump over fences, they will also find holes and tunnels to explore. This adventurer has found a hole in a wall.

Dogs need time to adjust to their new life and it takes at least three weeks for the real dog to emerge. A dog in the wild would not throw himself into a new pack or group; he would follow and observe, just as we take our time in joining in with people we don't know very well. After three weeks he will begin to feel more confident and at six weeks he will change again, and at each change you will think that finally he is settling but it will take a year before you look back and realize that each change was just another step towards you and your dog fully understanding each other.

Keen to investigate further, he is determined to go as far as he can and has pushed his body into the gap.

The nervous dog

A nervous or frightened dog will need a lot more than a few days to settle. If he is not used to being on a lead, walking near traffic or meeting strangers it can be weeks before you can take him out for a walk. Don't try to rush him: he will be fine with garden exercise for as long as it takes for him to have enough confidence in himself and in you to be able to venture further. It is important for him to feel safe and safety begins in the home, so a Dog Den in a quiet place is essential – and if he wants to spend most of his time in there to begin with, let him. Take him out into the garden regularly to encourage him to be clean but don't try to train him – he needs to feel free from any kind of pressure. If he doesn't eat to begin with, don't worry. Make sure he has access to water, and he will eat when he is ready and feeling more settled. If you panic and keep changing the food you are offering in the hope of tempting him, you may think you are being considerate to his needs but he will pick up on your inconsistency and interpret it as insecurity on your part. If he is so nervous that he tries to hide when he is out of his Den or in the garden, keep a light house lead on him so you can direct him to where you want him to be, and back again, without having to try to catch him.

Don't worry about what you should be pro-

viding for him, such as toys, lots of exercise and games with a ball. Contrary to the belief that Border Collies have to be mentally stimulated all the time and need endless exercise, they are actually the masters of down-time; although they need a sensible amount of exercise, your new dog will not suffer if you don't take him out on a long walk in the first week or longer. In fact, taking a nervous dog out too soon is more likely to be destructive than constructive. If he's never seen a ball before he is likely to think you are throwing it at him and not for him, and not being able to play with a ball or not understanding the game is not a major catastrophe. What your nervous dog needs is an endless supply of time and patience. If he's not used to a lead, begin at the very beginning, just as you would with a puppy, and if he's not house-trained don't panic or jump to stop him if you see him starting to soil in your home; accepting that you should have been a little more vigilant is far better than frightening him with your sudden movement. Dogs are clean by nature and if you use a Dog Den he will soon become clean, but if you don't and he regularly soils your floor he will take some convincing that he can't carry on doing it there and must learn to go outside. In your mind you may expect that

All that can be seen is the white tip of his tail and that will soon be lost from sight. A dog doesn't have to escape to disappear, and what may at first seem like an adventure to a dog can soon turn into a frightening situation. It's much better to keep a long lead on and keep your dog safe.

once he's settled he will learn to go outside, but in his mind he is being clean by not doing it in his bed. It won't occur to him that you don't want him to do it on the carpet as that isn't where he sleeps.

The 'Chill Mat' can help your nervous dog to settle but don't force him onto it and don't try to introduce him to it before he is ready and willing to sit at your feet.

The wilful dog

You may choose a rescue dog who has more attitude than nerves but he still needs the same start in your home as the nervous dog. In fact, showing him round your home and taking him for a long walk on day one will make him think he has an empire to try to rule. A headstrong dog needs to understand his boundaries on day one and to have them extended slowly and with control.

Lead walking is important for a strong-minded dog as he needs to know from the beginning that

he is not in control of a walk. At the same time, just as with the nervous dog, rushing things can cause more problems, so start slowly, using your garden, and only taking him where it is quiet and not until he has been with you for quite a few days.

The 'Chill Mat' is important for a strong-minded dog as in the first few weeks he will try to test any boundaries you give him, and when he does this you need to be able to calm him while you show him what you expect from him as acceptable behaviour.

THE FIRST FEW WEEKS

The 'Golden Seven' tip in Chapter 3 is just as relevant for a rescue dog coming into your home as it is for a puppy. The day you bring your rescue dog into your home is the first day of the rest of his life; although he has a past, his start with you needs to be as secure and consistent as you can possibly

Spend time in your garden with your dog just watching him and letting him get used to being in your company. The first time you can let him off the long line in the garden and he is relaxed and happy is an important milestone.

Don't wait until there are lots of distractions to try to build your relationship with your dog. The more time you can spend together, getting to know one another, the quicker you will become best friends.

make it. He will spend his first three weeks with you observing and either testing you or keeping out of the way depending on which type of dog he is. The second three weeks will be spent trying to persuade you to let him have his own way, or a nervous dog will be coming out of his shell. As he goes towards the end of his second month with you he will either have realized that you are his leader and parent figure or, in the case of a nervous dog, he will be beginning to realize that you can be trusted. If in those weeks you put pressure on your dog, whether he is wilful or nervous, you could find you have pushed him too far, causing the settling-in period to take much longer. He needs that time to observe, to settle in, to trust and to learn about you and your routine; it's a period of time he needs to go through and if he misses something because he's been rushed, he will end up reverting back to what he has missed.

For example, if a dog is nervous of going into the garden in the first few days and he's pressured by being taken out regularly and given treats while he's there, rather than allowing him to observe and feel safe, he may be persuaded to endure the garden but at some time he will revert back to being nervous of it. To have the courage to be able to face anything he is wary of, he first needs to be able to trust you, and that takes time.

However good your dog may seem on a lead and at coming back when called, you still need to keep him on a long training line for at least the first three weeks, and in some cases much longer. In that initial period a strong dog who has been really good to begin with will still be finding his feet and will test the boundaries, whereas the nervous dog needs to know you will always be there for him. If either dog runs off out of sight, they will be lost in an unfamiliar area.

MANAGING PROBLEMS

No dog is perfect, and it's often the little imperfections that endear them to us, but sometimes what begins as a shortcoming can grow into a problem that becomes anything but endearing. Most behavioural problems stem from something in a dog's past, either an incident that has left a deep-seated emotional issue or a habit begun during the formative years that has grown out of hand. For example, allowing a puppy to jump up at people may seem harmless at the time, but when the puppy becomes an adult and jumps up at everyone he meets, then it becomes a problem – hence the reason for teaching puppies to seek permission to greet people. A little extra time spent at the beginning of a dog's life can prevent problems when he becomes an adult. When a dog has stored a certain emotion or act in his memory, it will always remain in his memory bank and will be triggered by an action, a smell or a sound. To manage and control the problem you must try to avoid the triggers, or intercept the undesirable behaviour with acceptable behaviour, and in order to push the unwanted memory to the bottom of his memory bank you need to keep the bad memories dormant and add an abundance of positive actions or smells.

Jumping up

Border Collies are very quick to learn but they need simplicity; the more complicated the training, the longer it will take for them to forget the old and learn the new. The calmest way to teach a dog not to jump up is to create a controlled situation rather than wait until one arises; you need to be able to concentrate 100 per cent on your dog, with no distractions. Enlist the help of a friend. As they approach you, stand your dog behind you as in the lead walking safe position; your body language is then telling your dog that he is second in line and not number one. Run his lead (it must be on a normal collar and not a slip lead) under your foot and bring the lead up towards you. You are not upsetting or distressing your dog; he does not have to lie down or sit – he simply cannot jump up. If you bombard him with words he will ignore them as he will com-mit himself to jumping up, but if you take away the option to jump up while telling him what a good lad he is and then let your friend stroke him while he is standing, you have a dog who gets the attention he wanted but in a way that is acceptable to everyone concerned. When your friend stops stroking him, turn and walk away in order to defuse any sudden urge your dog may have to jump up when you remove your foot from the lead. After a few lessons you can begin to introduce him to other people and in other situations, and with patience the result is a happy dog who receives attention but has learned in a very gentle way how to behave – and people will want to meet and make a fuss of him.

Separation anxiety

No dog should be left alone for long periods of time but a dog who becomes fretful or anxious each time you leave the house is probably suffering from insecurity. Just as a child should feel safe in the home, so should a dog, but it isn't as easy to explain to a dog that the home is a protected place. You can't tell him with words, so you must show him with actions. First of all, check your dog's diet as excess energy can exacerbate some problems and will make an insecure dog even more nervous. Dogs are gregarious and love company, dog or human, but they are also good at switching off and relaxing on their own – but only if they feel safe. If your dog sees you as being below him or an equal partner then he is responsible for himself and the home area, but if he understands that the area is managed by you then you are responsible for him and the home, which will make him feel safe. Introduce him to a 'Chill Mat'; used correctly, it will teach him that the home is yours and he has his own areas in it, but you don't need to leave it down when you go out. Make sure he has a bed or a Dog Den and give him something to keep him content while you are out; some dogs do feel safer in a Dog Den but it must be in a place away from windows and doors. Don't make an issue of going out as you will only reinforce his concerns, but don't leave him for too long and when you return tell him what a good lad he is. Never ignore him. Making a dog feel secure needs a holistic approach, which means taking stock of everything he does or doesn't do. Good lead walking, recall, diet and boundaries are paramount in helping a dog to feel secure and settled.

Dogs on the furniture

Before you start changing rules or bad habits for a dog, you have to see life through his eyes. If he has always sat on the sofa but you buy a new one and want to introduce a new rule, you must remember that each day you are planning, buying and looking forward to your new furniture he is blissfully unaware of your intentions. If you have just brought a rescue dog into your home and in his previous one he slept on the sofa, he will see no reason why he can't do the same with yours. You can't change rules overnight for a dog without causing him some distress, so you need to look at what you want of him and then work out how to explain it to him in a way he understands. First of all, put a lead on your dog and when he attempts to jump up on the sofa ask him to sit down or to stand still, put a throw on the sofa, then invite him up. This way he isn't having a hard change of rule that he doesn't understand, your sofa is protected and a new rule is being introduced gently. If you do this each time he will begin to see that he is on the throw and not on the sofa, and he is being invited up and not taking it as his right to be there. Once he has this rule in his head you can go to stage two, which is asking him off the sofa and putting the throw on the floor for him to sit on. If your dog does get on your sofa and sleep there and you don't mind, it is still better to use a throw (technically, when visitors sit on the sofa they are in his bed, and you wouldn't let

them in his dog bed so why can't he be annoyed or jump all over them if they sit on his sofa?). By using a throw you are lessening the chance of any problems or confusion arising later.

If a dog has been used to sitting on the sofa and you want to change this habit, you can't just do it overnight. Start by putting a throw on the sofa and only allowing him on the throw; this way you are divorcing him from the furniture in favour of something of his own.

Once he gets used to sitting on the throw, and understands that he is only on the furniture when the throw is in place, he will sit on it on the floor and a new behaviour pattern will begin to emerge.

If you have a puppy and you don't want him on the furniture, then don't let him develop the habit. If you don't mind him being on the sofa with you occasionally, start him off with a no furniture rule and then allow him on with a throw as with an older dog.

The dog with no recall

The first few months of a dog's life can leave a lasting impression on him and a bad habit that persists uncorrected for months or years can become a way of life for a dog. Giving a home to a rescue dog carries a little of the unknown and if your dog has spent his life either running off or has been a stray living wild and looking after himself, you may find that teaching the recall will only ever give you 50 per cent of what you need.

If you have even a shadow of doubt about your dog's response to his recall, keep him attached to you. It is far better to know your dog is safe than to keep testing him by letting him have his freedom. Anyone who has lost a dog and spent hours searching and worrying, fearing the worst, will know just how heartbreaking it is to lose a dog even for a short time.

Border Collies were bred to work with man, not without him, so for them to be running with no guidance and no recall makes them isolated, and the one thing a Collie cannot cope with is isolation. Being left alone for hours can be torture for a Collie and whereas a young giddy one may become destructive, a nervous one will feel

---

DART THE RUNAWAY

Dart came into rescue when she was five years old and had spent her life going walkabout whenever she felt like it. Dart was given a job to focus on, and months were spent teaching her a recall. Most of the time she was a reformed character but every so often the wanderlust took over and off she went. She would stand calmly at her guardian's side in the house then suddenly turn a deaf ear and go. She would always go in a circle and would eventually make her way back home after spending time with local campers, rounding up a few sheep and trotting through the local village. Apart from the fact it was irresponsible for a dog to be running loose to go where she pleased she could have caused, or been part of, an accident. Dart spent her life on a long line when she was outside and was a very happy dog, accepting that while on that line she stayed with her guardian. This continued until she was too old to jump the garden fence but even then the gate had to be kept closed.

Dart spent the first years of her life going walkabout whenever she felt like it and she never really lost the habit.

THE MISINTERPRETATION OF 'RUNNING FREE'

The notion that Border Collies 'need' to run free is misleading. Certainly they need freedom to be dogs: they love to roll, graze, observe and hunt, all things we can provide while keeping them safe. To let them run loose without a proven recall may seem to be giving them freedom to run, but to the dog it is freedom to choose. When they are nearer to another dog, person or scent than they are to their guardian, they are free to choose not to go back.

Digby is deaf, so I have no means of calling him back to me if he goes out of my sight or crosses the line from my space to someone or something else. He never wants to be far from me and is a very happy, well-balanced, fun-loving dog who is good with other dogs and people. When people ask me how I trained Digby to be so attentive, they fully understand and agree that he has to spend a lot of time on a long line – yet they struggle with the concept of keeping their own dog, which has no recall, on a line – because he isn't deaf!

very alone. Running free with no control or guidance can be just as isolating as there is nobody on hand to help with any problem that may arise, and running with another dog when there is no control will take away the isolation but it won't provide the guidance they need. Seeing a dog enjoying the freedom to run is wonderful but you have to know that whatever happens you can bring your dog back to you with one call.

Chasing

Border Collies are sheepdogs and sheepdogs are trained to herd sheep, not chase them. It isn't a natural concept for a group of dogs to chase as they work together to hunt, pace, tire and catch their prey; if they chase it they either have to overtake it or hope it tires before they do. Dogs only know what they are taught and quite often they are, inadvertently, taught to chase. Throwing a ball for a dog to run after is telling him to chase something that is moving, catch it, bring it back and receive praise for it. Dogs chasing the water spray from a hosepipe, the wheels of the garden barrow or the brush are all receiving messages to the brain that to chase is fun and also acceptable behaviour. By the time they have progressed to cars, bicycles and joggers it is not acceptable behaviour and the dog has developed a habit that needs a completely new concept of how to play with a ball before it can be changed.

First teach your dog to sit calmly by your side. Still with the lead attached to him, roll the ball in front of you for a few yards but don't get him excited and don't use any words he will associate with running after the ball. Keep him on the lead and don't let him go for the ball until he is settled; it doesn't matter if he is sitting or standing, but you walk with him to get it. Progress will be slow but your aim is that he doesn't ever go

To teach your dog to wait, and to think before chasing after anything, use a ball to change his way of thinking. Hold him calmly on his lead, let him see the ball and then roll it a very short distance away.

Keep hold of him and keep talking to him, and when he has settled let him go to get the ball. If he is going to rush to it, keep him on his lead and go with him, keeping him at a steady walk.

after the ball until you have said he can, and the result will be that when something fires him up to want to chase he will be educated not to do so without your consent. The next step, still with the lead on, is for you to stop him halfway to the ball with a completely new word and then bring him back and tell him what a good lad he is, and then let him go and get it. Only do this once each session or he may decide not to go for the ball at all. The result you are aiming for is that if he does set off to chase, you have a special command to stop him en route.

Barking at strangers or other dogs

Whatever the reason an individual dog has for barking at the unknown, for example a past trauma or insecurity, barking dogs can be divided into two categories: headstrong dogs who want to check out who or what is approaching and take control, and nervous dogs who really don't want to have a confrontation and bark from fear to try to warn the other dog or person to stay away. Reading Chapter One should indicate which category your dog is most likely to fit into; for example, a very small, short-coated Collie with pricked-up ears and very light amber eyes is most likely to be filled with fear and want to run away, whereas a large black and white or tri-coloured collie with amber eyes will choose to be aggressive instead of running away.

The nervous dog needs to feel he is protected by you and the headstrong dog needs to know that you are in control, and therefore the one who makes decisions. Never allow a complete stranger to walk straight up to your dog; they are walking directly into his space, which can provoke a reaction of fear or of confrontation. Even if you know the person approaching, stand in front of your dog with a strong but not threatening body language; this blocks any energy or threatening scent reaching your dog, and also tells him that to get to him the approaching person or dog has to get past you first. It is a very simple body movement but it can prevent a nervous dog from feeling isolated and unprotected or a headstrong dog from believing it has the right to make decisions about how to respond to other people or dogs. The reason why some nervous dogs react less off a lead than on one is because off the lead they have the choice of flight or fight, but on the lead their only option is to fight if they don't feel their guardian will defend or protect them.

Dogs running loose

A well-behaved and well-mannered dog walking perfectly on a lead and with an excellent recall will not pose a problem to other dogs, but other dogs can pose a problem for him if they are running loose and are not kept under control. It doesn't matter how friendly the other dog's guardian deems him to be, he has no right to invade your or your dog's space without your consent. Accidents do happen where a normally well-behaved dog suddenly acts out of character and refuses to come back until he has introduced himself, but dogs who are continually allowed to roam free to approach anyone they meet are a problem. Not everyone is a dog lover and not every dog welcomes the advances of other dogs; if a dog is old, deaf or partially sighted he is at his most vulnerable when away from home and a strange dog comes near him. Once the other dog is nearer to you than to his own guardian he will have committed himself to keeping coming towards you so you need to take action before the dog gets too close to you; in most cases it is best to try to explain to the person concerned why you don't want their dog near yours. Should the intruder upset or frighten your dog, don't let him know how upset you are as this will only increase any fear he is feeling. Stroke him, tell him how much you love him and then carry on with your walk, talking to him in a confident voice. If possible, take him to somewhere he loves to be. If you take him straight home, the last thing on his mind at the end of his walk will be his reaction to the other dog. If you carry on or put him in your car and take him somewhere safer, then the last thing on his mind at the end of your walk will be what fun you had together. Think how you would feel if something really upset you and you went straight home to dwell on it, and how different it would be if someone took your mind off it and gave you something else to think about when you returned home.

Even if it is your favourite walk, if you see another dog approaching, on or off the lead, who appears to be threatening, don't wait to find out if it is – turn and go in the other direction. If it becomes a regular encounter, then for your dog's sake choose a different time to walk or find another route. Do not put yourself and your dog at risk.

Nipping and biting

Any form of nipping or biting should be managed before it gets out of control and turns into aggression. There are three types of aggression: dominant, nervous, and dominant born from fear, and there are three main reasons for a dog biting: protection, fear, or the belief that it is acceptable behaviour. Puppies are often excused when they display any form of nipping simply because they are puppies and are considered to be displaying normal behaviour. But just as it cannot be considered acceptable behaviour for a child to hit a parent, nor is it acceptable for a puppy to bite. They would not be allowed to bite their mother; they interact with their mouths but any form of nipping would be corrected immediately with a nip from mum. You cannot behave

in the same manner as your puppy's mum, you are not a dog and it is not acceptable to try to nip your pup. In your pup's mind he can interact with his mouth with mum and nip his siblings, so if you don't stop him from nipping you he will see you as a sibling or an equal, and as such has no reason to hold back from nipping or biting you. He needs to see you as a parent figure so you substitute the canine interaction of mouthing to one of stroking, which is both gentle and enjoyable.

The main reasons why a dog in a loving home may display aggressive behaviour can usually be traced back to the dog being destructive with toys, his bed, or even furniture, or chasing wheelbarrows and hosepipes, tugging and becoming generally hyperactive. Quite often the

Dogs with behavioural issues, or dogs who get over-excited, often seek relief from their anxieties and frustrations by chewing or shaking something, but destructive behaviour isn't acceptable, even with toys. One squeeze of a dog's mouth on something vulnerable can do a lot of damage.

leaning towards aggression isn't noticed until the dog actually bites someone and by that time the behaviour is well established. If your dog is a rescue you may not know what his triggers for aggressive behaviour are, and you may not even know he has them until he displays them while in your care. His general behaviour will tell you if he has been abused and is protecting himself by issuing a threat of being aggressive and willing to follow through, or if he is frightened and growling in the hope of warning you to keep your distance.

Whatever the reason for the aggression the first thing on your check-list is his diet. He needs to be on food that doesn't increase his energy levels. Next, assess his general behaviour towards you and other people or dogs. Is he frightened by them or is he aggressive towards them? A frightened dog needs to be kept at home and his trust in you firmly established; never try to make your dog 'face his fears'. Once he is feeling confident and trusts you, he will let you know when he is ready to move a stage forward. Treat each temperament or reason for aggression as if you are starting with a new dog: establish boundaries, give your dog his own space and implement the 'Chill Mat', and remove anything that winds him up or can instigate aggression. If your dog is food-aggressive be careful not to make an issue of it; the more important you make the problem, the more prominent it will become in his mind. Don't prepare or carry his food about when he is in the room; put it in his own area when he is outside and then bring him in and leave him to eat it in peace. Do not keep trying to remove it from him as he will see this as a threat and a challenge; once you have gained his trust and he knows you are not going to deprive him of his meal, he will allow you to move it if you really need to.

DON'T IGNORE YOUR DOG

To ignore your dog or turn your back on him is basically a snub, which is disrespectful and equivalent to treating him with contempt. You love your dog and want to teach him how to respond to you; treating him with indifference will lessen his respect for you, not gain it. There is a mistaken belief that this is pack behaviour but a pack is a family and no parent should ignore their child or their child's behaviour.

If your dog greets you when you return home, it is degrading and confusing for him if you ignore him. He needs either physical or verbal communication from you telling him how pleased you are to be back with him, and then you can ask him to wait or go to his bed while you do whatever you need to do. But don't ignore him.

If he is being annoying or jumping up at your visitors, don't ask them to turn their backs and ignore him. It isn't their job to train your dog and all he will learn is that he can pester them for a while until he gets bored. If you don't show him how you expect him to behave, he will never learn. Show him what you want as an alternative to the unwanted behaviour, but don't ignore him.

If your dog is pestering you to play with him one evening and keeps bringing you a toy, *don't* ignore him. If you do, he will carry on until he is bored, and then he will repeat the procedure the following evening. Ignoring bad behaviour and praising good is not a good balance; instead make it clear you want him to stop, sit him on his 'Chill Mat' and praise him. You wouldn't ignore a child so *don't* ignore your dog.

'NO' IS AN ACCEPTABLE WORD

You *can* say 'no' to your dog. In fact, you can say anything you want because he will only associate the sound with an action. It is a very misleading notion that it is 'negative' to say 'no' to a dog. It is meant to be negative! It is telling a dog to stop what he is doing but it should be followed by praise when he stops and listens to you. It is not the word that is important but the tone in which it is given, and if a dog is displaying unwanted behaviour then a deeper tone of voice is needed so the dog recognizes that you are not happy. It is not a growl or a threatening sound, but it has to balance the tone you give when you are pleased with him. If the words 'sit' and 'down' are taught to ask a dog to sit or to lie down, then it makes sense that he is told 'no' to prevent him exhibiting bad manners.

SUMMARY

If you introduce your new rescue dog to friends, family and other dogs too soon it can cause him distress and take him longer to settle in.

Behavioural problems stem from something in a dog's past and certain smells, sounds or actions can raise a memory for a dog that triggers unwanted behaviour.

Border Collies are not natural chasers; they are thinkers and strategists, but they are clever and love to please so your throwing a ball for them will make them think you want them to chase.

Ignoring a dog and his behaviour can make him feel insecure, whereas giving the dog an alternative behaviour teaches him what you want and gives him confidence.

METHODS

A rescue dog needs time to study you and his new home. Give him a quiet, calm place of his own and apply some basic good manners, but don't start training him or rushing him off to classes for at least six weeks.

Teach your dog how to play with a ball with some control, and use the ball to teach him how not to chase things that move. Instead, give him a game that means he has to use his mental energy rather than his physical energy.

If a dog cannot be trusted to come back when called, it is much safer for him to be kept on a long training line. He can have freedom to run and be a happy dog but he will be safe.

Solving any training or behavioural problems means taking the dog back to basics with the 'Chill Mat', lead walking and protection position.

If your dog is aggressive and you are nervous of him, seek professional help as soon as possible; he will know you are nervous and will take advantage of it.

CASE HISTORY – DANNY

Danny had been badly abused and when he came into rescue nobody could get near enough to put a lead on him. For several days I opened his pen door and let him make his own way to an indoor playpen to eat while I cleaned out his pen, changed his bed and then waited for him to go back to his quarters. I didn't rush him or try to make him do anything other than what he felt safe doing. It was three months before I could put a lead on Danny, with it taking all of ten minutes each time, and taking the lead off was even more testing. After six months in rescue I could put a lead on him and walk him out. Not once in that time did he show any aggression, simply because I never put him in a position where he felt he needed to be aggressive. The important thing we can learn from Danny's story is that we should avoid confrontation and be very patient in earning the trust of a dog because, whatever his problem, it was a human who caused it initially. Being patient with a dog and having him trust you is one of the greatest rewards. Danny is now in his forever home and is very loved.

Our beautiful Danny.

10 FUN WITH YOUR BORDER COLLIE

Border Collies are fun-loving dogs. They love to interact and they enjoy games that mean they have to think or work out a problem. The more you can give your dog to think about, the better he will like it and the more responsive he will be to you but if you keep repeating the same game with no variations he will soon become bored. Collies are like children – the more you teach them, the more they will want to learn, and don't underestimate their ability to work out a problem. You may be surprised by how quickly and easily your dog can solve what you may think is a challenge.

BALLS

Although ball-throwing can be fun, it is better kept to a minimum as endless retrieving of a ball doesn't offer any mental stimulation or challenge, and it can inadvertently teach them how to chase. Collies don't need much of an excuse to become over-excited or hyper, and young dogs need to avoid making sharp turns or jumping up for balls as their joints are still tender and they can damage their hips. Try to keep ball games involving excessive jumping or twisting to a minimum and concentrate more on games that combine fun with learning, something Border Collies love doing and do well. Instead of letting your dog run straight after the ball as soon as you have thrown it, make him wait a moment so that instead of chasing after it he sits and waits for your command to go, and then has to find where it landed. This is an excellent way of retraining a dog who does chase.

On a rainy day or a quiet evening try playing roller ball with your dog. Lie on the floor facing him with a ball between you and roll it gently towards him; if he tries to pick it up with his mouth, take it back telling him 'no teeth', and

One of Molly's favourite games is to find which plant pot the ball is under.

then roll it again. When he figures out that each time he uses his teeth to pick it up you take it back, he will try to think of another way, and after watching you for a moment rolling it under your hand he will start to copy you.

Let him see and smell a ball, and then place it under one of three plant pots. Shuffle them around and then ask him where it is. Don't wind him up to try to find it; once he knows it is under one of them, he will try to work it out but if you get him over-excited he will lose concentration.

Take a ball into the garden and tell your dog to stay while you walk round with the ball and quietly drop it under a bush or in some grass. If your dog has been watching you he will know where it is and go straight to it, making a 'find'. Once he has the idea of how to play the game, make it more difficult so that he doesn't see where you put it and has to use his nose to search it out. Most dogs love this game as they are using all their senses.

Whichever game you think would be really good to play, your dog's decision is final. If he really doesn't want to play a game or is unenthusiastic, then find another game or accept that he just wants to be with you and doesn't want to play games. You are doing it for him and to create a good relationship so you both have to want to play.

Tess isn't sure what she should do but is watching intently.

Tess is wondering what to do next and how to get the ball.

TOYS

There is an abundance of toys to choose from but your dog doesn't need a wide variety; in fact, he doesn't 'need' any of them, but using them to create a bond between the two of you can be rewarding as well as fun. But you don't need a toy box full and you do need to establish a few house rules, especially with young dogs: one toy at a time and no toys in the sitting room. A young dog will soon start pestering if he thinks your sitting room is his playroom, when in fact it is

She is looking very pleased with herself now she has managed to get it and is going to roll it back towards herself.

Tess still has possession of the ball but is wondering what the hand is asking for.

can actually over-stimulate a young dog and in some cases can exacerbate or even cause bad habits. Squeaky toys can really wind a dog up and if you have a young or problem dog who is shaking, chewing and ragging such a toy it is better to replace it with a calmer game. Toys that are designed to be filled with food may keep your dog occupied for a short while but remember that Border Collies are very clever and are always learning new things. Your intention is to keep him amused in the short term but his thinking will be more long term and the thought that food may be contained in toys can tempt your dog to try to get inside anything else he can find, which might include your best shoes! It can also increase the energy level of your dog's daily food intake if you are putting special treats inside.

Tuggy toys

Dogs needing to tug is another misleading concept, especially for a companion dog. Wild dogs tug to learn how to use their teeth, which is something a pet dog shouldn't know how to do. In some cases it is used to stimulate a dog into having more energy or is used as a reward, but unless your dog is being trained for a specific purpose, such as in the services, the use of a tuggy toy has no

where you take time out to relax. It is very easy to say to a child that it's time to put the toys away and settle down but for a dog what they do one day, or at a particular time of day, they think they can do any day and at any time.

It's worth bearing in mind that some toys purpose in your dog's life! He will start with a toy, then a tuggy rope; he will get wound up and may even growl when he's doing it. Next he will start thinking he can use his teeth on other things and may become destructive, or he may start tugging on his lead and trying to pull you

Tess has figured it out and with both paws is pushing the ball back to the open hands. As the game progresses, she will begin to push and roll the ball with her nose.

on a walk. He may even try to tug on something someone else is holding, thinking it a great game, but if they don't play it the way he expects he may become aggressive with them. You have a pet dog, a companion, and you want him to be safe and reliable around others and the last thing you want is your dog to think it is acceptable to use his teeth on anything connected to a human being.

Quotations from the old shepherds should never be dismissed. Border Collies are highly intelligent and often earn the reputation of being easy to train – and they are, once you understand them and learn how their minds work. Once something is in a Border Collie's mind, he will start to turn it to his advantage. When a dog is trained to work sheep, the shepherd will send him for a flock and leave him to work out the best way to bring them to him, allowing the dog to turn his knowledge to the shepherd's advantage. If there is no purpose for tugging and nothing constructive for the dog to gain from it, there is a danger that the companion dog will turn it into something he can do on his own.

MAKING TRAINING FUN

If Border Collies have a failing, it is their penchant for being obsessive, so anything new needs to be introduced in moderation and always in a stress-free area with no distractions. For example, don't wait until you are going out in your car to show your dog how you want him to travel: teach him at home and make it a game where he can work out what comes next. That way he has nothing to obsess over. Young dogs are better travelling in a crate or Dog Den and if they are used to one will settle quickly in a car. Don't let your dog jump straight in but ask him to wait and then give him a signal to jump in; likewise, ask him to wait before he gets out and get him used to sitting there with a door open. Teach this at home, and when he is comfortable with it start to use the slightest movement of your hands to signal what you want of him. He will love watching you and working out what you want from him, but don't combine words with actions once he understands what you want or he will expect to get both before he does as you ask.

Body language is one of the best 'toys' or 'tools' you can use to train your dog: it's free, it's fun and it's always available. Imagine how a deaf dog is trained: no words can be used and any fast or exaggerated movements will produce an anxious and nervous response. A deaf dog does not need to be focused all the time on his guardian but when they are in 'conversation' he will be looking for each movement he can recognize. Calling your dog at a distance needs a voice but when he is near you and looking at you a simple beckoning of your finger with no sound should bring him just as eagerly. Give a slight flick of your shoulder and see which side he comes to; walk towards him and then turn away and note his response. Try pointing to a ball and when he goes to it beckon him to come to you with it. Your dog will focus more on you and will 'work' at understanding you with an intensity you won't get if you are constantly repeating verbal commands. Just as your hands are for gentle and tactile reward and you should never use them to push your dog to sit or lie down, in the same way if you use your body language whenever possible, then when you do use your voice to tell your dog how good he is being, he may be more inclined to listen to you.

There is nothing wrong with using accessories such as balls and toys for interacting with your dog but be very careful they don't become an obsession for him, and try hard to use less of them and more of yourself for training him. Twenty minutes in the garden throwing a ball or Frisbee will tire him physically but it can also wind him up to the point of not settling when you take him back inside. In contrast, ten minutes of calm training and communication will give him something to think about and he will go back inside calm and responsive to you. So try to combine the two by playing with him for the first ten minutes and then follow up with some gentle body language movements to get him focused on you without being over-excited.

HIDE AND SEEK

Hide and seek is a great game to play. Start off at home so that he fully understands that you can

A game of hide and seek can be great fun, although while you're hiding don't let your dog out of your sight as you never know where he may go to look for you.

Hide and seek is fun and your dog might just turn the tables and hide from you!

be found and you are not leaving him, and get him used to tracking your scent. Begin by teaching him how to find or track a ball or toy, and then replace it with an item of your clothing (not a clean garment); drag it across the garden out of sight and invite him to find it. Once he is used to 'searching', put the garment on and hide. You may need to enlist someone to hold him for you until he gets used to the idea, but once he understands the game don't be surprised if he turns the tables and hides from you.

NOT ALL DOGS PLAY

Don't worry if your dog doesn't want to play; it may be because he is nervous and doesn't understand what you want. Give him time and wait until he has gained some confidence. You can start by just rolling a ball gently in front of him so he knows it isn't going to hurt him, and quite often his curiosity will get the better of him and he will start to interact with you. Some Border Collies just don't want to play and some will play

Not all dogs like to play with toys and some prefer to play on their own. Cody loves to throw things around and catch them on his nose.

Digby refuses to play ball with anyone but will play happily on his own, just rolling the ball around and squeezing it gently in his mouth. It's lovely if dogs can amuse themselves as while they are inventing their own fun, they are also getting the mental stimulation they need.

CASE HISTORY – BOBBY'S LAST CHANCE

As a puppy Bobby had played with toys and by the time he was a year old he had become destructive and was handed in to rescue because he was showing signs of aggression. Bobby ate his bed in the first week, shredded his vet bed and spent every moment he was on a lead trying to tug it out of my hand. If he saw a ball he would take it in his mouth and bounce up and down yapping at the same time and snapping if I tried to take it from him. Bobby was on a downhill slide and in danger of becoming very aggressive if he didn't get his own way. He was taken out of the kennels into a quiet area where he could settle, his toys were removed and he was walked several times a day on a lead (which he was not allowed to chew). He was an intelligent dog and soon learned how to walk nicely on a lead, and it didn't take long for him to

enjoy his recall as he got plenty of attention each time he came back. But Bobby was still manic if he got anything in his mouth, so he was taught how to search but instead of finding a search toy he 'found' another dog. (He loved other dogs but if he played with them he would become too rough.) When Bobby found his friend they would be taken on a long quiet walk together and on their return they would go into a paddock where they wandered around grazing the herbage and Bobby was taken back to his pen before he thought of play fighting. It took over a year before Bobby was able to be rehomed but he went to his new guardian able to walk on a lead, recall and with a lot of fun ideas such as 'high fives', 'speak' and 'roll over'. It takes a long time to turn round a dog who has developed such manic behaviour, yet a little control at the start of his life would have made such a difference. It needn't have changed *what* he played with, but it would have altered his perception about *how* to play with it.

Bobby had to learn a new direction in life – without toys.

quite happily but only on their own. It isn't the end of the world and in some respects they are no different from us. Some people love to spend their time outdoors doing energetic sports and some prefer to sit inside or in the garden reading a good book. Some people like hugging and being hugged and some prefer to keep their distance with just a handshake (and then only if they must). Just as we respect our friends' and families' different likes and dislikes, we have to respect a dog's preferences and not force our ideas of fun or play on to them if they really don't want it.

SUMMARY

Border Collies love to have fun and play but they get over-excited very easily and some toys or games induce unwanted behaviour.

Toys can be a valuable asset but they can also cause obsessive behaviour if they are used purely as a game and not as part of the development of your relationship with your dog.

If play sessions end on a high note with your dog over-excited and a little breathless the chances are that instead of settling when you take him home, he will get his breath back and still be very wound up.

Not all dogs want to play. Some don't know how to and some prefer to play on their own, while others will play to the point of becoming obsessed and don't know when to stop.

METHODS

Try to keep your dog calm when you are teaching him new things or playing with him, as he is more likely to take notice of you if he is not over-excited.

Use yourself to entertain your dog rather than relying on toys or balls all the time. Learning to watch your dog for his responses to certain movements of your body and then responding to his response is fascinating and really worth learning, as you will find out so much more about your dog.

Play games that make your dog use his brain rather than his body. Border Collies need exercise but too much too young can have an adverse effect on their joints, so play games that involve your dog having to work out a solution.

If your dog doesn't respond to anything you try, don't worry and don't write either yourself or him off as a failure. You are probably stressed about him and he is almost certainly waiting for you to calm down and stop trying so he can show you what he wants to do.

11 COLLIES, KIDS AND RELATIONSHIPS

Children can discover a lot about nature, compassion and relationships when they grow up with a dog, and it is good for them to be involved in the responsibility of looking after a dog and not just to see him as a playmate. However, a lot of thought is needed before bringing a dog into the family home for the first time as it is a huge commitment.

Children can learn so much from looking after a dog and Border Collies make excellent companions, but a dog needs to be taught how to behave around children and, in the same context, children need to know how to respect and behave around a dog. Learning how to behave with each other is important for both the children and the family pet, and although puppies are lovely and cuddly when they are small, they soon grow into big dogs. In the space of a year the little bundle of fluff that jumped up and clambered all over a small child and had a lot of fun will be a big strong dog, but the child will still be a small child and the game will no longer be fun. A dog-free zone and a child-free zone can save a lot of confusion. Yours will not be the only children in your home: they will have friends visiting, there will be parties and no matter how well you teach your children how to behave around your dog you cannot guarantee that other children will do the same. It is a good idea to have an area in your garden and a room in your house where your dog doesn't go; here your children can play with their friends, running around and making as much noise as they want but your dog isn't going to be getting wound up or misunderstood.

PLAYING WITH CHILDREN

Border Collies do not round children up thinking they are sheep! They interact with them, running

Children can learn a lot from living with and looking after a dog, and a Collie can be a great pal.

121

Border Collies do not round up or nip children mistaking them for sheep. Collies are bred and trained to be gentle. Here Glen is moving a lamb off a fence by pushing it with his nose and he is equally gentle with children.

Looking after their dog and helping to train him gives children a sense of responsibility.

AN ANCIENT BREED

The Border Collie is not a new breed. Its origins go back to farming and shepherding at a time when motor cars, four-track vehicles and quad bikes didn't exist, and where the local village and school were a good half hour's walk away. To the majority of the children of that farming era the Collies were their best friends: they shared secrets with them, they walked for miles with them and the dogs were their protectors.

excited, the game may turn into tagging with nipping, especially with young dogs. Children love being trusted and being important, and the responsibility of looking after a dog, rather than endlessly running around with him, can be the start of a beautiful friendship. There are plenty of calm games that don't encourage jumping or over-excitement to teach them how to play and enjoy each other's company, and encourage children to gently stroke rather than pat your dog. Children and dogs have the same uncomplicated outlook on life and once they become best friends they can share special moments that adults often miss.

VISITING FAMILY MEMBERS

Sometimes a well-balanced dog who appears to have no issues will act out of character and show a sudden reserve towards visiting family members; however, what may seem irrational to his guardians may seem perfectly logical to him. As

round and playing, almost like a game of tag. This is the sort of interaction they would have with other dogs and with their siblings; in the dog's eyes they are all equals. But if the game doesn't go as they intended, or if they get over-

Learning together how to play 'search'. A child who has a Collie for their best friend will never be lonely.

123

far as your dog is concerned, his family is the people he lives with, the people he takes his direction from, who feed him, love him and look after and protect him. If there is to be a next in line for him it will be a resident family member or a friend who visits regularly; to your dog there are no family ties other than regularity of visits or recognition of a familiar scent, and the latter is not easy for a dog to detect amid the vast range of surrounding scents and body perfumes.

Parties, special occasions, barbecues and festive holidays are great fun for families but mean nothing to your dog other than a lot of people in his home, some he knows and some he doesn't. He may be fine with this arrangement in general, but he may view things a little differently if a family member, who he doesn't see very often, stays over. When all the members of his family are together he may be fine with everyone, but on an occasion when only the visiting family member is present and perhaps tells the dog to go to his bed, asks him to sit down or tries to relieve him of a toy, your dog may think he is within his rights to refuse to take any notice and could even show some hostility. Whereas the human mind is thinking about everyone being related or very close friends and sharing their home and hospitality, your dog is seeing someone who may have been good fun during the day suddenly becoming all too familiar when they are not, in his eyes, part of the family unit. Most dogs will accept different situations and an extended family but if your dog is a little wary or acts out of character try to slip into his mind for a while and see the situation through his eyes.

A NEW FAMILY MEMBER

Preparations for a new baby begin months before the arrival but a dog also needs to be

A young dog can bring a new lease of life to an older dog, but don't let the young one push the older one around.

Once they become good friends, the young dog can learn a lot from his older pal.

Two dogs of a similar age can get on really well together but as one becomes a little more vulnerable the other can become a bully if any small arguments between them are not stopped.

prepared for the new family member. If he's not used to babies, or not being the centre of attention, it could come as quite a shock to him to be suddenly taking a back seat. Work out a routine for him that you will be able to keep to, and get him used to it before the new arrival. It won't be long before you have a toddler playing on the floor so try to have a dog-free area, or better still a play-sheet you can put down anywhere but that your dog is not allowed to go on or to take any toys from, and make sure your dog has his own 'Chill Mat'. A little time preparing your dog beforehand means that should he be a little too enthusiastic about the newcomer, there will be some boundaries he can understand.

A new adult member may also join a family unit and the dog who has enjoyed the constant attention and companionship of one person can feel resentful and jealous of a partner moving in. Once again, the dog needs to be prepared and accustomed to the new family member by going for walks and spending time on neutral ground, with the existing family member or members taking a back seat, thus allowing the new additional relationship to develop without jealousy or competition for affection.

Bringing another dog into the home can provoke jealousy in a dog who is used to being the centre of attention. If they are both young dogs they could soon get into arguments if they are not watched carefully.

LOSING A FAMILY MEMBER

Family circumstances change constantly. It's a natural progression: children go to school, leave school and eventually leave home. People marry, separate or get divorced; they may meet somebody else and remarry. People have choices and can make decisions, they know what is happening, they can prepare for it and they can prepare other family members for any changes. A dog has no idea: all he knows is that what was constant in his life has suddenly changed. The person or persons on whom he relied have gone and the emotions of those left behind will be confusing and maybe even distressing to him. This is the time when everyone is so busy trying to get on with their lives that they tend, for a time, to forget about the dog and his needs, yet this is one time in his life when he too needs support. He needs all the reassurance possible that whether the person he is looking for is or isn't coming back, he is just as much loved and as safe as he ever was.

OTHER DOGS OR PETS IN THE HOME

Older dogs often take on a new lease of life if a younger dog is introduced into the family, but it can also be very tiring for them. If a young dog is pestering an older dog, don't stand back hoping the older one will sort the problem out. He

These two are really good pals but not all dogs get on with cats and even a dog who has lived with a cat may not be so happy to live with another one.

needs you to make sure that the youngster learns to respect him and if the onus is on him to try to command that respect, resentment may arise between them that could prevent them from becoming friends.

Two dogs closer in age may be fitter and better equipped to sort out any differences between them by themselves but as the older dog begins to slow down he may become a target for the younger one trying to take over. You need to be aware of little subtleties, such as where bed sharing becomes bed owning by the younger one, or a simple collision in the garden causes a flash of temper from him, or he begins to step in front of the older dog, pushing him away from food or your affection. Never favour the youngster believing this will make him think he has won and will stop his bullying tactics. You wouldn't support a bullying child, so don't support a dog who becomes a bully. Instead, make it quite clear that you are in control. Use a separate 'Chill Mat' for each and make them both sit down quietly but not too near each other. If you favour either one of them, the other will harbour resentment but by getting them both to settle down near you they are both equal; neither is being placed above the other, the trouble-maker is being harnessed and the vulnerable one is being protected.

Cats

Not all dogs get on with cats, and Border Collies often like to stalk them. If they have not grown up with each other there is no guarantee that they will live together successfully, and much will depend on their individual characters. If the cat is young and likely to run away, the Collie will probably find it fun to give chase, while an older, more complacent cat may be content to just keep out of the way or to sit and ignore any advances your dog may make. Border Collies can be quite fickle in their choice of companions – they may be hostile to the neighbour's cat, yet curl up and sleep with the family cat. If one is an established part of the family and the other a newcomer, some firm rules need to be established and kept until you are sure what kind of relationship is going to evolve.

SUMMARY

A Border Collie will not mistake children for sheep and round them up but he can interact with them as he would with siblings, and dogs play strong physical games with each other.

The arrival of a new baby in the family can be a very emotionally charged time for a dog, and the attention the baby gets, plus the inevitable crying, can distress him.

People entering and leaving the family unit may be part of the family's plan but to the dog it is a complete surprise and in some cases a shock.

Bringing another dog into the home can provoke jealousy in the family dog, particularly if he is used to having plenty of attention and has been the only dog for a long time.

The 'Chill Mat' helped Sammy overcome his fears.

METHODS

Border Collies can make wonderful companions for children but, although they can be best friends, they are not playmates on an equal footing, and establishing child-free and dog-free areas can save a lot of stress, especially on the occasions when other children are visiting.

Border Collies have very sensitive hearing and the sound of a baby crying can cause them distress. It is inevitable that your dog's routine will change, so it is better to change it *before* rather than *after* the new arrival, giving him something familiar in his life to fall back on.

A dog can suffer just as much as any other family member if someone moves out of the family home. Make sure he has something each day to look forward to, have some compassion for what he is feeling – but don't overdo it as he needs as much normality as possible.

If a new member is moving into the family home, don't wait until near the event to see if your dog will approve. It's very hard to take a back seat with your best pal but you need to let him spend time with the new family member on neutral ground and be willing to hand over the lead a little and step back.

If you are bringing a new dog into your home, introduce them to each other on neutral ground and don't encourage them to approach each other directly. To give them the best chance of liking each other, let them walk together and get used to each other's scent. They need to weigh each other up before making contact only and when *both* of them are ready.

CASE HISTORY – SAM'S STORY

When Sam was a puppy he played happily with small children but at six months old he encountered some older children who upset him and he made it quite clear he didn't want to be near them. Sam was given his own place in the home and a 'Chill Mat', and no pressure was put on him to interact with the children. He soon learned that if he didn't feel happy all he had to do was sit on his Mat and he was safe, and the children knew never to go near him when he was on his Mat. When other children visited, he went to his own quiet area. Without any pressure on him he had time to observe and to get over whatever had made him feel so anxious. After six weeks he began to relax, and he would sit and watch the children playing, until eventually, and under supervision, he returned to the confident lad he had been before. While Sam was learning that not all children were upsetting, his family, including the children, were learning how sensitive he was and the value of allowing him time and space to work things out.

12 LOVING, LIVING AND LEARNING

Whatever you are teaching your dog, don't rush. Make sure you give him information he can understand, and give him time to absorb it. Whether he comes into your life as a puppy or a rescue dog, young or old, giving him time and patience will pay dividends. We all have an idea of what we want or expect from a dog, and it is very easy to rush through all the stages to try to achieve the desired result as soon as possible. It is much harder to stand back and be patient, to let him grow mentally and physically, and to

listen to what he wants, but that hard work and patience will be worth every minute of the time dedicated to it.

The first weeks and months with a new dog, young or old, are important. It's like getting to know someone you have never met before but want to get to know better. Each time your dog looks at you and responds to your voice or touch there's a magical moment of bonding, so rather

Creating the foundation of good manners training may sometimes seem like an uphill struggle . . .

. . . but it's worth every effort and ounce of patience it takes because when you succeed and get to the top of the hill you have the whole world in front of you and you can go in any direction with your dog that you wish to take.

SHEPHERD'S COMMENT

'Training a dog is like building a wall. You're not sure which stones you need, so you order a lot – some you think you need, some you will decide are not what you want and some will be maybes. You will be surprised how some of the maybe's become invaluable, some that you 'knew' you needed just don't fit right and the ones that you were going to throw out become indispensable. But whatever stones are right for you and your wall you need to spend time, patience and thought laying down the big heavy foundation stones, because without them your wall will always have flaws.'

Socializing with your friends and their dogs doesn't have to involve hour-long treks and games. Being able to enjoy a pleasant walk and then just sitting, relaxing and letting your dogs chill out in each other's company is good for you and your dog, and is what you have been working towards.

than looking at the formative months as a hurdle to overcome, see them as the foundation of a friendship that will last for a long time.

You don't have to go to classes, socialize, join clubs and associations, train for the disciplines and compete, nor do you have to walk miles every day come rain or shine. Border Collies have been around for many years and were in companion homes long before the Kennel Club recognized them as a breed, and certainly a long time before agility, fly ball and other dog-related pastimes existed. There was no need then for them to be anything other than a wonderful friend and companion, and nor is there now. They do need exercise and they do need mental stimulation but so does any other breed of dog. Some do need more than others, but Border Collies can suffer from over-stimulation. If you want to take your dog to clubs and competitions, don't take him as a bad-mannered youth. We painstakingly teach children good manners before they start school and a sensible, well-mannered dog will respond much better to further training than a dog with no manners. If you do decide you want to try any of the disciplines, or would like to compete, you will be proud of your dog when he is calmly and sensibly listening to what you want of him and enjoying doing the things you want him to do. But don't feel pressured into doing something because you have been given to understand that Border Collies must be 'doing'. Border Collies need understanding, and they need to feel needed; 'work' doesn't just mean being on a farm and working sheep, it means being a part of a unit and having a role to play. That role may be on a farm, or in one of the services; it may be in a sport or it may simply be as your best friend and companion, to go for walks with, to share happy and sad times with and to enjoy special moments together.

Good manners training will enable you to take your dog anywhere, perhaps to enjoy a nice relaxing social half-hour after a walk. There are children playing ball in the background and a group of people at a nearby table but the dogs are sitting quietly, relaxed and content, and not being a nuisance to anybody.

EXTRA SPECIAL DOGS

Every dog is special but some need just that little bit extra time, patience and care. They may be blind or deaf, have an illness, suffer from arthritis, or be elderly and in need of peace and a place to rest their head. Some of these dogs end up in rescue centres where they may be overlooked for a new home because they have a problem, yet each one of them is capable of leading a normal life and of doing what Border Collies do so brilliantly – giving. Like all Collies, they give their love unconditionally and ask only for a loving home and for someone to be their best friend.

Mossie was born deaf and partially sighted. She came into rescue at six months old and was the happiest little dog anyone could wish to meet, and she now has a wonderful loving new home. Joey has a rare form of diabetes and his sight is failing, but he loves nothing better than to sit and enjoy cuddles. Milo was in a road accident and had to have a leg amputated; he might

Mossie was born deaf and partially sighted but she was a happy little soul who didn't know any different.

With another dog to guide her and give her confidence, Mossie grew to be a wonderful fun-loving friend and companion.

133

Young dogs love to show off and Fred's supple young body is bounding with energy.

A leap of faith! Old Rob may not have as much energy but he still loves trying to be young again.

As a youngster, Hope never played with toys but as a more senior gent he took great delight in carrying them away from the younger dogs!

have only been able to sit sideways but having three legs didn't stop him from running around and getting the most out of life. Digby is deaf and the spoken word is of no value to him but body language and emotions make a lively form of communication to which he responds so well that he can work sheep.

OLD DOGS

Border Collies don't begin to grow up until they are two years old. By the time they are four they are beginning to settle into adulthood, and by the time they are ten they have learned so much that their retirement will never be dull. They are amazing, wise old dogs with a wealth of knowledge to draw from. Living with an old Collie is never dull and can be very humbling when day after day they continue to give their love and

SHEPHERD'S COMMENT:

'Old Fleet is that darn clever he can go out and bring every milk cow into the byre, then go back and take the sheep up the fells, all without a word from me. I swear the day they make the lids easy to take off the milk churns, he will be able to tip the white stuff in himself and will make me redundant.'

support, never once recognizing that they are actually retired and should be resting.

Border Collies really do live for the moment.

Border Collies are brilliant at entertaining themselves. These two cheeky chappies spent over fifteen minutes just watching a cat sunbathing!

Rob found it entertaining trying to reposition a Yucca plant!

They love the freedom of movement, yet they can stand in the stalk position without moving a muscle for as long as it takes for the target of their focus to move. They are clever enough to learn how to be assistance dogs, search and rescue dogs and of course they are amazing sheepdogs, yet they are sensitive enough to be Therapets. Border Collies are very sensitive, even the ones who appear to be strong and wilful, and they have a wicked sense of humour – why else would old Rob run off with a slipper and drop it in the stream, or try to stuff a Yucca plant down the toilet?! Yet when you are feeling down or sad, the Collie who has been driving you mad in some way or another will be there at your side, and you will feel his wet nose push into your hand and his paw on your knee. When you stop to wonder why he didn't jump up and wasn't his

Border Collies have so much to give, and the older they are the wiser they become. We can learn so much from these wonderful dogs.

Quiet moments and quality time: friends for ever.

usual boisterous self, you will realize that he was sharing your sadness; he was being there for you and he always will be.

Dogs give more than they take. We have so much to learn from them and each dog will leave us with something to take forward to the next dog and the next part of our lives. It is a shame not to take forwards what our dogs give us, because by doing that we are keeping their memory and what we learn from them very dear, and in so doing they will always remain a part of us.

THE GREY AREA

This is what you have been waiting for and have worked towards. You have put in the hard work and been patient, you have listened to your dog, watched his body language, learned how to understand what he is saying, or is about to do, and you have learned to communicate with him. You are inside his head and you can understand what he is thinking and why, so now you can switch off and enjoy the relationship you have with him. You no longer have to worry if he is going to be frightened or confrontational with another dog or a person because he knows you will sort out any problems. You no longer have to ask your visitors to sit quietly while you teach your dog how to behave, because he now sits at your feet and would rather be with you than the visitors anyway. You don't have to keep putting the 'Chill Mat' down each evening because he doesn't need to keep being reminded to settle down. You don't have to worry about him chasing things because you've taught him how to have fun without chasing. The world is your oyster – you can take your dog anywhere and in any company, you can train for competitions or you can take him running or cycling with you. There is nothing to stop you being as energetic as you want, or instead you can go on leisurely walks and simply enjoy each other's company. Never forget to tell him how much you love him and don't ever get tired of stroking and massaging him. Even Collies who are not very tactile love to have communication; eye contact and a gentle smile will tell them that all is well, and for them that can be the equivalent of a hug.

You have an amazing dog: intelligent, loving and sensitive. Love him, be patient with him and always try to see his point of view. Never be afraid to try to work out what he is thinking and why; you will be surprised how much you can find out and how willing he is to share his feelings with you.

If you aren't afraid of a challenge, are willing to be patient, have a good sense of humour and love the intelligence, grace and sheer beauty of the breed, you will always have a Border Collie at your side and you will have a friend who is loyal beyond compare and loves you unconditionally.

FURTHER INFORMATION

USEFUL WEBSITES

Mainline Border Collie Centre
www.bordercollies.co.uk

Freedom of Spirit Trust for Border Collies Rescue
www.fostbc.org.uk

International Sheep Dog Society
www.isds.org.uk

BOOKS

McCulloch, John Herries *Sheep Dogs and their Masters* (Toft East Publishing)
A history of the Border Collie and their remarkable lives

Sykes, Barbara *Understanding Border Collies* (Crowood)

INDEX

RELATED TITLES FROM CROWOOD

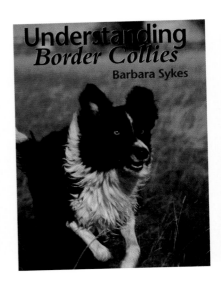

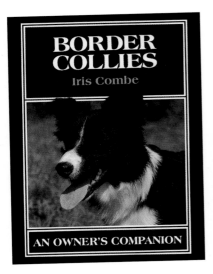